OCD

For Teens And Adults

Mindfulness, ERP, Brain and Other CBT Strategies
To Manage Intrusive Thoughts and Compulsive
Behaviors

BILL ANDREWS

CONTENTS

INTRODUCTION

Imagine having to live life in a perpetual state of fear and anxiety, with your mind never at rest. Think of yourself in a state where you never do anything but worry about your thoughts and the fearful feelings they bring. How would it feel like if you lived a life that doesn't really feel like a life? Not many friends, no social life, no career, no relationships, just you and some thoughts that make your heart race its fastest when they come to mind. Oh wait, you probably don't have to imagine because this is already your reality as it is the reality for a whole lot of people.

Obsessive compulsive disorder "OCD" may seem like a fancy word to throw around for some people but for people like you who have to live with this terrible disorder, you know how devastating it is to even live with something as terribly dreadful as OCD. Although it was originally considered a rare disorder, the reality is over 2 million teens and adults now live with obsessive compulsive disorder in the United States.

OCD is a mental health condition that places a person in a cycle of extreme distress and certain ritualistic behaviors. It can hugely interfere with the functioning of a person's life and their physical, mental, and emotional health. Unfortunately many people with this disorder, they don't even know that is a disorder, something to be worried about. For those who know this however, they have no idea about what exact steps to take and how to go about recovering from and removing OCD from their lives.

If you are currently reading this, then it means you are one of those people who wish to recover quickly from their OCD and start living a healthier, anxiety-free, positive, and happier life. Thankfully, you can count yourself lucky because you don't have to look any further. This book "**OCD For Teens And Adults**" is the ultimate guide you need to master your thoughts and emotions so you can recover from obsessive compulsive disorder.

This book has been written to help people suffering from OCD get rid of intrusive thoughts, feelings, and compulsive behaviors so they can create a life of genuine happiness, peace, and calm for themselves. This is a must read because it will take you through your recovery process by starting from the very basics of OCD to the modern treatments and medication available to help you in very simple language so as to make everything easy to comprehend.

From a look at the history of OCD to the types of OCD and the most effective techniques for combatting obsessive thoughts and compulsive behaviors, we will go into depth on everything you need to know about OCD and how to completely recover from this disorder. More importantly, you will also learn about how you can employ mindfulness meditation practice, exposure and response prevention (ERP) , and other cognitive behavioral therapy techniques to project yourself into a life of clarity, happiness, and positivity.

CHAPTER ONE:

AN IN-DEPTH UNDERSTANDING OF OBSESSIVE COMPULSIVE DISORDER (OCD)

Nowadays, OCD as an acronym has been romanticized in an almost fashionable way. You hear someone saying either, "Oh, I'm so OCD," or "Wow, Lillian is a little OCD." The reason for the romanticism of OCD isn't farfetched. Many people believe that OCD pertains to being extremely neat, tidy or sometimes fussy. It somehow seems like most people forget that OCD is a disorder and a mental disorder at that. As a person who is suffering from obsessive-compulsive disorder, you definitely understand the fact that OCD goes way beyond the tidiness or whatever childish meaning people have ascribed to it.

Due to this popular misconception of OCD, it is only fitting that we begin the chapter by trying to understand what a disorder is. After all, how can you understand the severity of obsessive compulsive disorder if you don't even know what 'having a disorder' means? In a very simple definition from the Oxford English Dictionary, a disorder is regarded as "an illness that disrupts normal physical or mental functions." From this definition, one thing that should be instantly clear is that disorders are abnormal and dysfunctional. Disorders impair the functioning of a person's life to the degree where their mental and physical health are adversely affected. From all conceptions, obsessive compulsive disorder checks the boxes for all the criteria of something that affects mental and physical functioning and therefore qualifies as an abnormality, something that needs to be corrected. Having said that, let's move to understanding what obsessive compulsive disorder really is!

Twenty-five years ago, psychologists believed Obsessive Compulsive Disorder (OCD) to be an incredibly rare condition that could only be found in a small number of people. Thanks to new discoveries, technology, and treatments though, it has now been established that OCD actually affects millions of people across the globe. According to published statistics, almost 1.2 percent of Americans suffer from OCD and a slightly higher percent of these are women. Thus, it is a quite common mental disorder that a lot of people battle with. It is difficult to understand what exactly prompts the repetitive thoughts and uncontrollable behaviors that characterize OCD. So, for you to understand what obsessive compulsive disorder really is, it is only necessary for us to look in-depth into what OCD is, the cause, and the symptoms to help you self-diagnose whether you are a person with this disorder.

Obsessive compulsive disorder is a mental health disorder that involves having a plethora of recurring/unwanted thoughts, urges, and images (obsessions) that invade an individual's mind, causing mind-boggling anxiety and distress and compelling the individual to engage in certain repetitive behaviors (compulsions) aimed at reducing the anxiety and discomfort being felt. Often, these compulsive behaviors are acted out in an almost ritualistic and specific way; they are never random.

As humans, most of us have a cycle of focused, recurring thoughts and some behaviors that we constantly repeat. But, these thoughts and behaviors don't have an impact on our daily life or affect its structure in a negative way; they may even be geared towards making our daily activities and tasks easier and more routine. For people who suffer from OCD, these thoughts are neither focused, wanted nor geared toward helping to achieve any meaningful thing; they are usually quite disturbing, persistent in an annoying way, and not acting on them results in distress, anxiety, and depression.

For instance, it's normal to make a habit of double-checking whether you have unplugged the iron from the socket on occasion; but, it becomes a compulsive behavior when you let this habit mess with your mind and disrupt your daily life to the point of distress. Normally, people with OCD feel compelled to perform certain actions in a repetitive and ritualistic manner out of the fear that something may happen if they don't; this fear stems out of the intrusive and uncontrollable images they conjure in their head recurrently. If you are afflicted with OCD, there is the chance that you recognize that you have obsessive thoughts and compulsive behaviors, but you find it difficult to restrain yourself and keep the thoughts out of your head. The way OCD works is that your brain gets stuck on a particular image or thought which compels you to repeat an action over and over. For instance, your brain could conjure an image of you getting infected with germs so you constantly wash and rewash your hands more than 20 times in a day to ensure this doesn't happen. Although this action doesn't necessarily provide you with a sense of enjoyment when you perform it, you are relieved of the anxiety which is or would have been generated due to the intrusive and obsessive thoughts you have.

There are two participatory themes in obsessive compulsive disorder as evident from the name, and these are:

- Obsessions

- Compulsions

Obsessions, in the context of this mental disorder, are recurring and persistent urges, impulses, images, or thoughts that provoke emotional distress and anxiety. They are excessive, unnecessary and you have no control over them. Many people with OCD recognize the fact that these urges, thoughts, and images are unreasonable and illogical products of the mind, yet they are unable to break free from the hold they have on their consciousness. Some people try to stave off or suppress these obsessions with other unrelated thoughts and actions but this usually doesn't work. Typical obsessive thoughts include concerns about safety, harm, or contaminations, a need for perfection, balance, or exactness, and out-of-bounds sexual thoughts.

Compulsions, on the other hand, are repeated and continual behaviors, which an individual feels driven and compelled to perform in response to intrusive and uncontrollable thoughts, urges, or impulses. Compulsions are usually performed to minimize or prevent distress or anxiety. In extreme cases of OCD, these compulsions are sometimes performed consistently in a ritualistic manner such that it becomes impossible to have a normal routine. The anxiety caused by these obsessions and compulsions is further worsened by an individual's knowledge of the fact that they are excessive and irrational. Acting out the compulsions often brings about some momentary relief from the anxiety; however, the obsessions come back and this becomes a cycle that is repeated again and again. Examples of compulsions include cleaning the house over and over to reduce the fear of contamination, checking the stove again and again due to a fear that the house may burn down, repeating certain phrases or names to safeguard against suspected injury or harm. There are even severe cases of OCD where some people repeatedly retrace a driving path to ensure no one has been hit or injured. There are people who refuse to shake people hands at social gatherings just because they have imagine these people to be filled up with germs waiting to contaminate them; OCD is as serious as this. Generally, OCD is known to begin in people from teenage years to adult ages. It is an especially common mental disorder among teenagers and it often manifests in different types, which we will of course, be discussing in a subsequent chapter.

Understanding OCD completely would be quite impossible if we don't take a look at the history of this disorder, which is a quite interesting history, by the way.

THE RELIGIOUS AND MEDICAL HISTORY OF OCD
Obsessive compulsive disorder was once known as 'obsessive compulsive neurosis' but before it came to be known as that, its history was seated deeply in religions. OCD as a disorder is quite common and it covers a broad spectrum. It would be no fallacy to say that OCD has existed right from when people started existing. Right from the beginning of time,

many people experienced issues of obsessions and compulsions even though they probably didn't register as a problem then. From research, it has been established that there have been historical descriptions of what is now known as OCD as far back as the 14th century. While the disorder did not come to be known as OCD until the 20th century, that doesn't dispute the fact that many people have experienced symptoms of OCD since a long time ago. In fact, OCD then was simply known by the term "scrupulosity."

Early descriptions and recognition of OCD are found in the religious literature, without any record in the medical literature until the 18th century or so. Around the 14th century, people experienced obsessional fears pertaining to religion and this made the word "scrupulosity" become a thing. Obsessions and compulsions were later to be regarded as symptoms of melancholy around the 17th century. In the modern day, scrupulosity is used in psychology to refer to obsessive concern with personal sins and a compulsive performance of religious rituals to depict devotion. However, back then in the 14th century, this word was simply used to embody all forms of obsessive thoughts and compulsive behaviors. Around that time, scrupulosity was so common especially in religion, that people were warned against being 'too scrupulous.'

The first public representation of what we now

know as OCD was made by John Moore in 1691 when he recognized that there was something called 'religious melancholy' in people. He preached about religious melancholy using examples of morality worshippers who are constantly tortured by blasphemous thoughts no matter how hard they try to suppress these thoughts. According to report, he described these "scrupulous" people as having a defective fear of their thoughts and how they make them unworthy to be in the presence of God. He also talked about how no matter how hard these people tried to stifle those thoughts, they simply grew stronger and struggled more. Moore further preached that most of the people who have these thoughts were good people, because bad men would never even have these thoughts in the first place.

From every indication, Moore had simply preached about what we now call OCD. Like we said, much of the descriptions relating to OCD were found in religious literature. This comes as no surprise since religion was a core part of everyone's life then and OCD mostly centered on things that are the most important to an individual. From history, it wasn't unlikely for a person with defects or illness to go to their religious leader for a cure or treatment. These religious heads and figures often became acquainted with varying health issues due to the interactions they had with parishioners. In the 17th and 18th centuries, physicians started to observe more forms of compulsive behaviors which included washing, checking, and fear of sickness. Religious obsessions were noticeably starting to fade out now because they were no longer as prevalent as they were in the earlier centuries.

Around the 19th century, concepts relating to OCD became more modern. Physicians sought to understand whether OCD was a disorder of intellect or emotions. A French psychiatrist known as Jean Etienne Dominique Esquirol concluded that OCD was partial insanity, a form of monomania. Since Esquirol was unable to tell whether OCD was a thinking disorder or a volitional faculty disorder, the idea of OCD being a form of monomania was abandoned in the 1850s, and French psychiatrists further sought to understand OCD within broader categories which are now identified as panic disorder, phobias, manic behavior, etc. Henri Dagonet, another French psychiatrist, suggested that OCD was a form of impulsion, impulsive insanity to be specific. Impulsive insanity is a form of mental illness in which violent, irresistible impulses led to obsessive and compulsive behaviors. Again, another French psychiatrist named Benedict Augustin Morel described OCD as a disorder of the emotions. Morel believed that OCD was caused by a pathology affecting the nervous system.

Around the end of the 19th and 20th century, Gregor Mendel made a discovery of related genetic principles, making a number of concepts about

OCD and degeneration come into play. Valentin Magnan, a French psychiatrist even described OCD as a psychosis of degeneration. While French psychiatrists were busy with the emotive and volitional theories, German psychiatrist and neurologist Wilhelm Griesinger proposed that OCD was a disorder of rumination. Another German psychiatrist countered this and described OCD as a disorder of intellectual function.

To warp up the history, behavioral psychology and cognitive psychology started to gain ground in the 1970s and they overcame every other theory that tried to explain OCD. To date, behavioral and cognitive psychology are the best models for understanding OCD and what it entails. Although there have been no causes of OCD identified by science, we will be looking at some of the factors that could contribute to the development and maintenance of OCD as we progress in this book. The history of OCD can be better understood when you look up early cases of people who were thought to have had obsessive compulsive disorder in the past. They include: Martin Luther King, Charles Darwin, Nikola Tesla, Howard Hughes, John Bunyan, and many other well-known people. Kindly read up on them if you feel up to it!

A DEEPER LOOK AT OBSESSIONS AND COMPULSIONS

As you already learned, obsessions and

compulsions are the two main recurring themes in Obsessive Compulsive Disorder. The aim is to better understand what obsessions and compulsions are so you can understand how they are entwined in OCD.

A recurring theme for everybody with OCD is the experience of unwanted thoughts which are referred to as obsessions. These thoughts are usually uncontrollable, persistent, and disturbing. Sometimes obsessions come in form of images, fears, impulses, or a combination of all three. You never invite obsessions, they just come barging into your mind when you least expect it, and this is one the reasons why they are regarded as intrusive thoughts. Although most people experience intrusive thoughts and they are normally able to wave them away as fast they come, people with OCD find it incredibly difficult to ignore these thoughts, making them a major hindrance to optimal daily functioning. Obsession as a word was derived from the Latin word "obsidere," which means "to besiege."

This is exactly what people with OCD experience with intrusive thoughts; they are *besieged* by these thoughts, making it almost impossible for them to find a way out. Expectedly, the victim of these obsessive thoughts does not want or welcome these obsessive thoughts because they are very disturbing and they bring such pain and despair with them. Often, the sufferer will go to any lengths to resist or control these thoughts. Invariably, they often come rushing back in minutes, hours, or sometimes days, leaving the sufferer mentally frail and exhausted. As a person with OCD, you might always know that your obsessive thoughts are illogical and irrational, but the fact that they feel very real and make you give certain emotional and physiological responses makes you believe the plausibility of these thoughts.

One thing to note about OCD is that these obsessive thoughts never go away; they are repetitive and you literally have no control over their generation. All intrusive obsessional thoughts produce feelings of unease and distress, which most people describe as a trigger of anxiety. For many people, obsessions go hand in hand with thought suppression. Since obsessions are literally the main theme around which OCD revolves, experts have suggested that thought suppression may be the reason for the recurring of obsessions in OCD sufferers. Naturally, as humans, when we encounter unwanted thoughts in our mind, the natural reaction is to try to suppress these thoughts so as to push them away from our consciousness. However, the thing about these thoughts is that they are just as stubborn as you are. The more you try to push them away, the harder they come back, even worse than before. Without doubt, this makes you want to suppress even harder and before you know it, you are in a vicious, distressing cycle with obsessional thoughts.

In a particular study, OCD sufferers were instructed to resist and suppress their obsessional thoughts on certain days, while allowing themselves to have these thoughts freely on other days. They were further asked to record the number of obsessional thoughts they experienced in a journal at the end of each day. At the end of the study, people with OCD found out that they recorded more intrusive thoughts on days they tried to suppress the thoughts than the days when they allowed the thoughts to run free. This goes to prove that obsessions become more obsessive as a result of people with OCD trying to suppress them.

Compulsions are repetitive mental or physical actions that an OCD sufferer feels the urge to perform in a purposeful and almost ritualistic manner. In clearer terms, compulsions are behaviors you engage in over and over and over without break. A typical occurrence with compulsions is that the sufferer almost always feel a sense of resistance towards the action but this is usually overshadowed by the strong drive which fuels the compulsion. Often, compulsions are performed in order to provide relief from the distress and discomfort brought about by the obsessional thoughts. While some people may be able to resist the urge to perform a compulsion for a short moment, they find it ultimately impossible to completely override the urge or control it.

Compulsions are typically targeted at getting rid of the feelings of fear and anxiety that come from having obsessional thoughts. They are also performed to eliminate a possible harmful situation such as the death of a family member or friend. People with OCD often know that their compulsive actions are unrealistic and illogical but they feel compelled to perform them anyway, just to ensure they are not being idle or leaving their thoughts to come to pass. For example, some people start counting numbers in a specific pattern when they have a thought about a beloved family member dying. When you think about it, counting numbers won't actually do anything but they do it anyway. If you are an OCD sufferer, then you surely know in a way that your compulsions will do nothing to stop or affect the imagined situation, but you can't fight that need to carry out the compulsion anyway.

Compulsions are either overt or covert. Overt compulsions are the ones that are observable by other people -- like when someone keeps going to the door to check that it's really locked. Covert compulsions, on the other hand, are those actions you carry out mentally, meaning someone else can't observe them. An example is the repetition of certain phrases in the mind. Covert compulsions are also referred to as cognitive compulsions since they are acts performed in the mind, like a thought.

Most people tend to confuse obsessions and

compulsions, especially as pertaining to their connection to OCD. On their own, obsessions and compulsions are both disorders. This makes many people assume that they are somewhat alike. The most obvious difference between the two is: obsession has to do with cognition while compulsion has to do with behavior. An obsession involves recurring and persistent ideas or thoughts while a compulsion involves recurring and persistent actions. In other words, you think obsessions while you act out compulsions.

There are also people who sometimes mistake compulsion for addiction. While both terms share certain similarities, there are key differences to watch out for. Addiction has to do with the dependence of a person on a substance or behavior in order to manage or cope with their life. In time, the dependence they have on the substance or behaviors becomes so important that they continue to engage in the use of that substance or persist in engaging in the behavior, not minding the harm it brings to them, their loved ones, and other important aspects of their lives. In contrast, compulsion is simply an irresistible and intense urge to perform an action, which sometimes leads to a behavior but other times does not. Compulsions are a minor and major feature in both addiction disorders and obsessive compulsive disorders respectively.

The key difference between addiction and

compulsion is: Addiction involves pleasure while compulsion doesn't. People with OCD don't do certain things because they gain pleasure from it; they do it due to distress and despair. There is no pleasure when OCD is involved.

Next, let's look at the major cause(s) of obsessive compulsive disorders and the symptoms with which you can identify if you or someone around you suffers from OCD. Has the cause of OCD been recognized? What is (are) the identified cause(s) of OCD? What are the symptoms and signs that point to an OCD tendency in people? These and many more are the questions to be answered in the chapter to follow.

CHAPTER TWO:
THE CORE CAUSES AND SYMPTOMS
OF OCD

Over the years, researchers have tried to identify one or more definitive causesof OCD but there have been no causes identified. Experiencing intrusive thoughts is a normal thing for everybody, but most people are usually able to dismiss these thoughts from their consciousness as soon as they come along. However, when it comes to OCD, people get stuck with the intrusive thoughts, unable to get rid of them from the conscious mind, which makes them become overwhelmed.

Experts have suggested that the main cause of obsessive compulsive disorder may be the fact that the brain of people with OCD functions differently from that of a normal person. Thanks to neuroimaging technologies, evidence has been provided to show that some areas of the brain function differently in people with OCD compared to people without the mental illness. According to research, certain symptoms of OCD may be due to communication lapses or errors among some parts of the brain like the thalamus, cortex, striatum, and etc. Some abnormalities also occur with the neurotransmitter systems, which include chemicals such as dopamine, serotonin, and glutamate that are responsible for relaying messages between brain cells and this may also be part of the cause of OCD in patients.

While there have been enough research evidences which show that obsessive compulsive disorder has a neurobiological basis, there has been no specific cause or causes of OCD found in patients. Several theories have also been propounded in the bid to identify the definitive cause(s) of OCD, to no avail. However, experts believe that OCD symptoms may be the result of a combination of different factors like neurobiological, cognitive, behavioral, genetic, and environmental causes.

Before we move on to discuss how these different factors could result in OCD symptoms and the theories that have been propounded to back them up, it is important that you understand that they are just theories and you can't really tell what exactly is responsible for your OCD. Many explanations have been developed by people trying to understand the roots of OCD. Some people believe that OCD is inherited while others argue that major life experiences, usually traumatic, may be the root of OCD. There are also people who believe that OCD happens as a result of a chemical imbalance in the brain. Researchers and experts however agree with some theories more than others. Nevertheless, let's discuss each of the possible causes of OCD one by one and understand how they are likely causes.

- **BIOLOGICAL FACTOR**

  Based on research, some experts have argued that OCD is a result of chemical imbalance in the brain; this is linked to genetic or biological factors. Several neuroimaging research studies have consistently provided pictures of brain scans to show that some areas of the brain works differently in individuals with OCD, yet there has been nothing to show how those differences in the functioning of the brain actually relate to the symptoms of OCD. Initially, in neuroimaging scans, it was shown that blood flow patterns are different in people with OCD compared with controls, and the basal ganglia and cortical cerebrum are the most affected by this difference in blood flow patterns.

  However, meta-analytical studies following that have also established that the differences between OCD patients and controls were consistent only in the caudate nucleus and the orbital gyrus. This means that it may be normal or expected for people with OCD to have different brain activities when compared to people without OCD. The thing about brain and neuroimaging scans is that they are affected by varying patterns of activity in the brain and so, are able to identify differences in how it reacts to different situations. Therefore, the parts of the brain that work differently in people with OCD simply get activated when there is a situation or environment causing an OCD patient to suffer. This makes it unsurprising that there would be different brain activities between people with OCD and people without. So this doesn't prove that OCD is indeed a biological disease.

- **GENETIC FACTOR**

  Studies on genetics establish a tendency for anxiety to run in certain families, although this may only be slightly. Some research conducted in the past have also established the likelihood of an individual with OCD having someone else in the family with OCD or some of the other disorders categorized under OCD too. Based on the results of meta-analysis studies conducted in 2001, individuals with OCD are 4 times more likely to have another family member with OCD compared to someone without the disorder.

  This, together with other studies, have made researchers recognize the possibility of genetic factors being the cause of OCD, showing that there may be the possibility of a familial connection in OCD. However, despite tons of studies conducted to support this, there has been no evidence to show that genetics may be a definitive cause of OCD. Interestingly, many OCD patients also don't seem to recognize anybody else in the family with OCD or other anxiety problems.

What this means is that genetics may not be the cause (or the only cause) of OCD and that the familial connection to OCD may be the result of learned behaviors from the family environment. So, while genetic factors may not be completely ruled out as possible cause of OCD, you should also know that this may be due more to environmental factors or learned behaviors.

- **CHEMICAL IMBALANCE**

  Some theories suggest that symptoms of OCD may be credited to an imbalance in serotonin, a neurotransmitter in the brain, and many mental health professionals also agree with the possibility of this being an OCD cause. Serotonin is a chemical in the brain which is responsible for sending messages between brain cells and neurologists believe that it is responsible for sleep, memory, and anxiety regulation. The theory about serotonin being the cause of OCD is based on the discovery of how the effective serotonin active tricyclic antidepressant clomipramine didn't affect the serotonin, early in the 1960s.

Initially, researchers argued that there was a major deficit in the production of the serotonin but there was nothing to support this suggestion. Then, it was suggested that the serotonin has subtle abnormalities that were responsible for OCD but again, nothing served as evidence for this claim. Recently though, researchers have suggested that the proof of the plausibility of the serotonin theory is the particularity of serotonin reuptake inhibitors and selective serotonin reuptake inhibitors medication. But, since this was the initial observation that led to the development of the serotonin theory, scholars have agreed that it isn't enough proof to establish the cause of OCD.

However, one thing to keep in mind is that OCD sufferers often experience relapse with the withdrawal of SSRI medications, especially when there is no behavioral therapy already set in motion. This proves that while serotonin may not be an actual cause of obsessive compulsive disorder, it may be a major reason why OCD persists in patients since it is an important neurotransmitter performing specific functions.

- **BEHAVIORAL FACTOR**

  In the 1950s and 1960s, two patients with chronic obsessional neurosis were successfully treated. Chronic obsessional neurosis was the original name for obsessive compulsive disorder. After that, a series of other successful treatments were also reported. The successful cases resulted from the application of psychological theories to obsessions and also the discovery of how behavioral treatments could be effective for OCD treatment.

  Subsequently, researchers proposed that compulsive behaviors were learned and in fact, were 'learned avoidance.' Note that behavioral therapy was already being used successfully for the treatment of phobic avoidance patients but it wasn't proving as effective in the treatments of obsessions and compulsions. Thus, researchers suggested that it was important for psychotherapists to combat avoidance behaviors by making sure compulsive behaviors did not happen during treatment sessions.

  This led to an anticipation of a cognitive approach to tackling OCD since that emphasized the part the expectation of danger or harm played in obsessions and how important it is for these expectations to be invalidated during therapy sessions. However, experts concluded that this was less important to the main objective of totally preventing compulsive behaviors. Around the early '70s, some researchers also developed treatment methods that involved exposing OCD sufferers to situations they are fearful of. The results of this research and approach were included in the Exposure and Response Prevention (ERP), which is a highly effective behavioral treatment. The ERP treatment method garnered major support based on a number of experiments that showed that when a ritualistic behavior is provoked but no ritualistic action actually takes place, the urge to perform the ritual immediately subsides.

Thus, the behavioral theory of OCD is based on the observation that obsessions become associated with chronic anxiety through conditioning. These researchers argue that OCD sufferers have developed certain avoidance behaviors, which makes it difficult for anxiety to be eliminated. So, ERP works by exposing the person to whatever provokes the obsession and then, helps the patient prevent avoidance so as to escape the compulsive response. More importantly, the discovery that obsessions often lead to heightened anxiety and compulsions led to further attenuation of anxiety, made a significant contribution to the development of ERP. When compulsions were prevented, OCD sufferers experienced a decrease in the level of anxiety and the urge to perform the ritual. With continued practice and experiment, anxiety was completely eradicated.

These early experiments later set the stage for the development of Cognitive Behavioral Therapy, which we will discuss further in a subsequent chapter.

- **COGNITIVE FACTOR**

  The cognitive theory of OCD was developed by researchers based on the argument that OCD sufferers have dysfunctional beliefs that lead them to misinterpret intrusive thoughts, thereby resulting in the development of OCD. The cognitive model of OCD states that humans experience the occurrence of intrusive thoughts occasionally, but people with OCD have an inflated sense of responsibility which drives them to misinterpret intrusive thoughts as being significant, resulting in huge consequences.

Furthermore, the model argued that continued provision of relevance to intrusive thoughts resulted in the development of obsessions and since intrusive thoughts usually bring distress, individuals with OCD often end up engaging obsessive thoughts by performing the compulsive behaviors in a bid to resist or block the obsessions. In a way, this led to the development of the cognitive behavioral therapy, which focuses on how people attach meaning to internal or external events. Cognitive behavioral theory was built on the behavioral theory due to its argument that obsessional thoughts are rooted in intrusive cognitive processes. However, the cognitive behavioral theory proposes that the difference between normal intrusive cognitive process and obsessional intrusive cognitive process is in how people with OCD interpret the context of the intrusive thoughts, rather than the intrusive thoughts themselves. For instance, if interpretation focuses on harm, anxiety would be the likely emotional response.

Cognitive behavioral theorists therefore suggested that obsessions may be normal but they become problematic and dysfunctional when an individual interprets the occurrence or context of the obsessions to be significant, meaningful or threatening and this is what leads to a distress response in the form of anxiety.

- **PSYCHOANALYTIC THEORY**

  Initially, this theory was believed to hold some form of truth but recently, it is being disregarded as a possible explanation for the development of OCD. The psychoanalytic theory argues that OCD happens as a result of a person being fixated on conflicts or traumatic events experienced in childhood or how a child interacted with the parents while growing up. However, since psychoanalytic therapy has failed to successfully treat cases of OCD, this theory is now being disregarded as a cause of OCD.

- **STRESS AND PARENTING STYLE**

  Another factor that has been recognized as a likely cause of OCD is stress from parenting styles, but no evidence supports the possibility of this. Stress is not a definitive cause of OCD but it may be a trigger to OCD. Major stressors and traumatic experiences in life may precede the development of OCD in patients. However, this doesn't mean they actually cause the disorder. However, they may trigger OCD in an individual already predisposed to it. When left unchecked, stress and normal anxiety may heighten the symptoms of OCD in a person.

- **DEPRESSION**

  Without evidence to support it, depression has also been identified as a likely cause of OCD. But, it is more likely for depression to worsen symptoms of OCD rather than be a definitive cause. In fact, many mental health professionals argue that depression is a causal state from OCD rather than the cause of it.

From all we have discussed, we can conclude that a range of these factors all contribute to the development of OCD but none is actually the definitive cause of the disorder. Experts believe that the likely cause of OCD may be a combination of more than one of these different factors.

Obsessive compulsive disorder doesn't just happen at once; it starts with a range of symptoms and sometimes, these symptoms even appear to be perfectly normal behaviors. Recognized OCD symptoms include:

- The fear of dirt and germs: You are often afraid of touching things others have touched. You also avoid hugging or shaking hands with other people.

- Washing and cleaning: You repeatedly wash your hands or take a bath.
- An illogical need for orderliness: You become distressed when you see objects out of place. You have a need to arrange things in a specific way, especially at home.
- Order: You try to eat certain foods in a particular order and you arrange your belongings in a certain way.
- Checking: You always check repeatedly to ensure that the door is locked or the stove is off.
- The fear of harming yourself or others: Thoughts of harming yourself or another person often pop up in your mind, even when you are thinking of something unrelated.
- Counting: You often find yourself counting numbers out loud or to yourself in a specific pattern.
- An unexplainable fear of making mistakes: You always need reassurance or encouragement from people around that you are doing something right or the exact way you should.
- A fear of being embarrassed: You are scared of behaving poorly in social situations.
- Routine: Before exiting your house or office, you do certain things a specific number of times in a certain way.

- A fear of having evil thoughts: You often conjure disturbing sexual or disrespectful scenes in your head.
- Hoarding: You like to collect things you don't actually need and you can't even seem to stop buying these things.

Sometimes, the routines you engage in have nothing to do with the obsessive thoughts you are having and you may take hours getting them done, thereby disrupting other activities you should have spent that time on. To confirm if the disorder you are really suffering from is OCD, you would have to visit a trained psychiatrist for further diagnosis. A formal diagnosis will include: Blood tests and psychological evaluations to check your blood count, the state of your thyroid, and presence of certain substances in your system, and your feelings, obsessions, fears, compulsions, and behaviors respectively.

Normally, many people experience superstitions and have fears that they may have left the door unlocked or the iron on when going out. If you have these thoughts but in a logical way, it may not be OCD. However, if you can't control these thoughts and they take up at least 60 minutes of your day and even generate problems for you in life, then this may be pointing to OCD and the need for professional help.

TYPES OF OBSESSIVE COMPULSIVE BEHAVIORS

Obsessive compulsive disorder comes in different forms, some of which are related to the symptoms we just checked out. It is not uncommon for an individual to suffer from more than one of the OCD forms, but OCD patients usually suffer from a specific form of OCD.

OCD symptoms vary from person to person, which is why there aren't technically any types of OCD. However, obsessive compulsive disorder is classified based on common symptoms which are described as types. Although patients experience specific symptoms in a relatively stable way, there is often a change in the nature of symptoms. So, although you may have majority of symptoms that are linked to a specific subtype, it is also possible for you to experience symptoms of other OCD types.

From a perspective of what causes or drives OCD however, psychologists agree that OCD may be categorized under two broad umbrellas, namely: OCD driven by fear and OCD driven by nervous system discomfort. Therefore, we will be discussing the two major types of OCD and the symptom subtypes of OCD respectively.

- **OBSESSIVE-COMPULSIVE DISORDER DRIVEN BY FEAR**

  This type of OCD involves a patient performing compulsive behaviors or rituals as they are also called as a result of the belief that if they don't perform this ritual, something bad or dangerous (usually the things they are scared of) will actually happen to them. For instance, an OCD sufferer who is scared of coming to harm will constantly do things like checking kitchen appliances repeatedly to ensure a fire breakout doesn't occur and harm them or their loved ones.

  There are OCD sufferers who also have an obsession with health due to the fear or germs or sickness. These people believe they or people close to them will fall sick if they fail to do some things and take certain actions. For people who are scared of contagion they exhibit this fear by compulsively cleaning surfaces based on the beliefs that they or some other people could contact germs from the surfaces and get sick.

  That's not all. Some individuals with OCD also have a fear of the intrusive thoughts which continually occupy their minds. Intrusive thoughts usually involve the thoughts of harming themselves, other people, or a fear of breaking common rules. It also involves uncomfortable thoughts pertaining to their romantic relationships. For instance, an individual with OCD may have thoughts of incest, bestiality, pedophilia, sexual aggression and other wild, sexual themes. Naturally, anybody can have these thoughts randomly but with OCD, the person has a strong fear that these thoughts may be a representation of whom they really are.

To find relief from these thoughts, people with OCD driven by fear would often engage in some specific actions repetitively, similarly to people with harm obsessions. In other cases, they would simply engage in mental rituals which may include counting certain numbers or repeating certain words in their head, using a certain pattern. In situations or cases like this where there is actually no ritualistic behavior involved, the OCD may be referred to as "primarily obsessional OCD" or "pure OCD."

- **OBSESSIVE-COMPULSIVE DISORDER DRIVEN BY NERVOUS SYSTEM DISCOMFORT**

  In 2005, it was discovered by the Behavior Therapy Center's researchers that some people actually experience OCD symptoms similarly to people with Tourette syndrome. People with Tourette syndrome has a problem with the nervous system which prompts them to make short involuntary movements or sounds. Therefore, these researchers suggested that Tourette OCD (as they named it) can also be driven by a nervous system problem. Individuals with this type of OCD often feel the need to perform a ritual over and over even when there is no actual reason why they should do this ritual. They usually do it only because not doing it leaves them in an uncomfortable state.

  People with Tourette OCD, as named by the researchers, have no idea why some things bother them; they often describe this state as "not just feeling right." Their OCD is not because they have a fear that something dangerous or harmful would happen if they fail to perform an action.

As we have said, OCD is also categorized as symptoms subtypes since the symptoms usually vary from patient to patient. They include;

- *CHECKING*

  As we already identified checking as one of the symptoms of obsessive compulsive disorder, the "checking" OCD subtype is one of the most common form of OCD in patients. Checking OCD has to do with a compulsive behavior of checking something repeatedly to ensure it is the way it should be. It includes actions such a locking and unlocking the door repeatedly or switching a kitchen appliance on and off to ensure it is really off. To normal people, this kind of action may seem ridiculous or outright amusing. But, to a person suffering from the checking OCD, the action is driven by fear and anxiety and it is usually to a point where it affects their lives.

  For instance, a person with "Checking" OCD may engage in locking and unlocking the door for several hours, making it difficult and almost impossible for them to maintain functional relationships. Some of the symptoms to check out for this subtype of OCD include: checking of the appliances, wallets, water taps, light switch, and door and windows repeatedly. People with checking OCD may also exhibit other obsessive behaviors like: checking in on family and friend repeatedly, reading documents over and over to ensure they contain nothing offensive, repeatedly reading up and researching on symptoms of an illness, and other obsessional behaviors driven by fear.

- **COLLECTING OR HOARDING**

This is another subtype of OCD based on the symptom of patient collecting and keeping old and new items even when the patient doesn't actually need these items. It recently became a widely popular subtype of OCD due to the rise in number of shows portraying this type of OCD. Hoarding OCD involves being unable to discard old items which are no longer needed, a compulsive need to collect a whole lot of useless objects and items in the house, and an inability to actually organize and arranges these items in an orderly way. Individuals with "Hoarding" OCD always have homes filled with plenty old or new useless items to the point where they only have a small space to manage in their house. This type of OCD is driven by the nervous system since the collection and hoarding of items is actually not done out of fear, but out of a need to just do it. The items being hoarded usually range from decayed or decaying food, old plastic bags, old newspapers, and sometimes, human waste.

Hoarding OCD is a specifically dangerous type of OCD because it exposes the sufferer to possible health risks. The unhygienic and confined environment which occurs from hoarding may lead the person to contract varying diseases, some of which may be chronic or fatal. Beyond the issue of hygiene, the house where the hoarder lives may be difficult to move through, thanks to the confined space. In a case like this, if a possible fire outbreak happens at the hoarder's house, he or she may be unable to get out quickly due to the piled up objects and items in the home. Hoarding OCD can further be broken down into 3 sub categories which include: sentimental hoarding, deprivation hoarding, and hoarding to prevent harm to others.

Sentimental hoarding happens when there is an emotional significance attached to every item, making it difficult for the OCD sufferer to get rid of the items. Sometimes, the OCD sufferer may even believe that getting rid of these items may make the memory associated with it fade away quite easily. Deprivation hoarding involves the inability to discard items due to the belief that they may be needed in future, not minding how unlikely that is. Hoarding to prevent hard to others is when an individual with hoarding OCD refuse to get rid of harmful items such as shattered glass or human waste because they believe that doing so may cause harm to others. Even though this is illogical, the hoarder is basically trying to protect others without minding the harm it is doing to them.

- **CONTAMINATION**

  If you are a fan of the movie "Matchstick men," then you probably already have an idea of what contamination OCD is all about. Contamination subtype OCD has to do with obsessions that cause to perform compulsive actions such as washing yourself and your environment over and over to an unhealthy point. For example, a person with contamination OCD may buy a large amount of hand soaps and use a new one every time they have to wash their hands. This kind of OCD is driven by an extreme fear of contracting diseases or infections from germs that may clinging to surfaces around the environment. People with this OCD subtype often make great efforts to avoid contact with people, going outdoor, visiting public restrooms, hospitals, or restaurants.

  There is also a subtype of OCD known as mental contamination. Although it is almost the same as the physical contamination, the difference is in the fact that the individual with this OCD has an obsession with internal uncleanliness, instead of physical germs. In several cases of this type, the uncleanliness is usually causes by psychological hurt. As an example: if someone with this type of OCD is publically disgraced or ridiculed by another person, they may spend hours and hours washing their body and trying to get rid of the ridicule. Here, it is the emotional abuse which leads to the compulsive behavior, not the fear of germs or dirty surfaces.

- **RUMINATIONS**

  Just like cow ruminates on cud, people with rumination OCD suffer from never-ending ruminations. The word rumination was derived from a Latin word "ruminari" which literally means "chewed over," which is exactly how an OCD sufferer literally chews and chews on chains of thoughts, usually negative and completely unproductive. However, these thoughts may not necessarily be intrusive or objectionable. Instead, the OCD sufferer chooses to spend hours and hours of their day indulging these thoughts instead of repressing or fighting them back.

  There are also OCDs that deal completely with intrusive thoughts only. Unlike rumination, this type has to do with thoughts that are highly disturbing and nearly distressful. They are involuntary thoughts, unwelcome and are usually about just any topic. They usually center on topics such as sexuality, relationships, religion, and magical thinking. Examples include constant doubt of a partner's fidelity, fear of being attracted to kids, thoughts of carrying out violent acts on innocent people, etc.

SIMILAR CONDITIONS TO OCD

Although OCD was once categorized under anxiety disorder, it is now recognized as a single, full-blown disorder with its own related conditions. These related conditions are not types of OCD but they share similarity and some symptoms align. Some of the related conditions to OCD are;

- Trichotillomania: This a hair-pulling disorder that is characterized by an individual's need to compulsively pull out their hair. It is usually difficult for this urge to be control, causing serious hair damage and loss and a major recline in social functioning.
- Body dysmorphic disorder (BDD): Body dysmorphic disorder causes obsessions with appearance, especially perceived flaws in the appearance. Usually, such flaws are minor, skewed, non-existent and unperceived by other people. A typical BDD sufferer spends a lot of time using makeup and doing other stuffs that improve their appearance. They may even go the length of getting plastic surgery.
- Excoriation disorder: Similar to Trichotillomania, this is a skin picking disorder in which the sufferer has a compulsive need to pick at the skin. It usually causes heavy damage to the skin and may also affect social relationships. Sometimes, it also results in skin infections.
- OCD caused by medication or medical conditions: This is a completely different

category of OCD which is caused by substance abuse, medication for another condition, or another medical condition in itself.

It is vital that you don't mistake these other conditions for OCD or vice versa. No matter the type of OCD you suffer from, one thing you should know is that it all starts from the brain and your mind. While some people argue that the brain and mind are one, it is important to state that they are two different things. Therefore, we shall be examining the link between your brain, your mind, and yourself next!

THE IMPACT OF OCD

In pop culture, the media often downplay the negative impact of OCD such that many people even label themselves as being OCD. Obsessive compulsive disorder is portrayed as a quirky, cute positive disorder but those who actually suffer from this disorder understand the many adverse effects it has on their lives and relationships. OCD has devastating effects on the sufferers.

Thankfully, OCD is a treatable illness but nevertheless, it would be outright negligent if we don't touch on the impact and effect of OCD so we can further help people understand that OCD is not something to make a joke or cute trend of. Out of all the population of people suffering from OCD, about 50% actually suffer from a severe case of OCD while less than a quarter of the population deal with milder forms of OCD.

According to the World Health Organization (WHO), OCD is one of the top tem most destabilizing illnesses in terms of quality of life and earnings. WHO also reported that this same OCD is a leading cause of disease burden among women aged 15 to 44. For this exact reason, it can be terribly disheartening when you see people make light jokes of this condition or describe themselves as being "so OCD" while ignoring the fact that OCD is a disorder and also ignoring the fact that it has devastating impacts on the life of people who have it in their lives.

The severity of OCD is such that it affects major or all areas of life of the sufferer. It can completely mess up a person's education, self-development, employment, career opportunity, personal and professional relationships, and quality of life. Certain compulsive behaviors which OCD sufferers have to contain also have a lot of harmful and negative impact which include physical damage and substance abuse.

OCD affects people in various ways. Depending on the severity of the condition, some people may spend the day carrying out different compulsions, making them unable to go out of the house or engage in their normal routine. Others who are able to go about their normal routine still have to cope with these obsessions and this usually have a hugely stressful toll on their lives. Other people carry out compulsions in secret and most time avoid social interactions and activities so they can get the time to complete their compulsions.

Evidently, the severity of OCD varies from person to person. There are people who are able to hide their OCD from loved ones and these people are usually the type who engage in covert compulsions i.e. mentally observed compulsions. Notwithstanding, the disorder often has huge negative impact on their social relationships, resulting in frequent conflicts and discord. In some cases, this may even lead to major things like divorce or separation. The disorder may also affect the person's ability to work, study, or engage in social activities.

OCD can be especially difficult when the sufferer can't even recognize the fact that they have a problem. In these cases, the individual will find it almost impossible to recognize the excessiveness of their concerns and worries. They may not even know that they have OCD and need to seek professional help. Reports also show that OCD may affect the financial state of a family.

Conclusively, in rare cases, OCD even directly affects family members of the sufferer more than the individual himself. For instance, a person with contamination OCD may set extreme hygiene measures in place and this may end up affecting the health of family members. The impact OCD has on family members of sufferers cannot be overemphasized. Sometimes, the family members and loved ones often get stuck in the cycle of OCD compulsions too. This especially happens when they are aware of their loved one's OCD. They may try to play their part by;

- Giving reassurance to the sufferer
- Avoiding triggers of loved one's OCD
- Unwittingly carrying out compulsions for their loved ones in a bid to ensure they don't have to do all that themselves.

While we cannot disregard the adverse impact OCD could have on the quality of life a person leads and the relationships they keep, we must also note that successful treatment can help an OCD sufferer move on from the OCD and start leading a more qualitative and improved life.

In the next chapter, we will try to look inside the mind of a person with OCD in order to understand how it actually works. If you are the one with OCD or your loved one is, understanding how it works in the mind is crucial to learning to manage and treat obsessive compulsive disorder.

CHAPTER THREE:
THE MIND AND BRAIN:
UNDERSTANDING HOW OCD WORKS

From the title, you probably think this chapter just wants to talk about the relationship you have with your mind and body as a person. In a way, you may be right. However, this chapter is more concerned with the relationship you have with your mind and brain as a person with obsessive compulsive disorder. In this chapter, we aim to look in-depth into the mind and brain of an OCD sufferer and understand what goes on in there exactly so we can better understand this disorder.

Firstly, are the mind and the brain one and the same or two different entities entirely? Some people argue that the brain and mind are different; these people are dualist. They are of the opinion that the mind and brain are made up of completely different stuff. When you have this kind of opinion, it becomes almost impossible for you to comprehend the nature of consciousness. Every day, we read of some brain diseases causing mental disorders and dysfunctions. One thing many people may not agree with is the idea that the brain and the mind are one. The mind represents a state of consciousness but where does consciousness really come from? The brain. Your human brain is the seat of all activity going on in your head.

According to Psychology Today and Jacob Sage, consciousness may be aptly viewed as "the ability of the mind to acquire information and all the content that the information contains and the ability to get the information in and out of memory." When you see a red cap, you immediately identify it as a red cap because your brain already knows that it is; you don't need anything else to identify the red cap. Therefore, your brain is identical to your conscious mind. The purpose of this is not to give a materialist against dualist argument, but through the course of this chapter, we will be recognizing the brain and the mind as one in the bid to understand what happens inside the head of an OCD sufferer.

One thing central to OCD is intrusive thoughts and these thoughts are usually conceived in the mind. The thoughts may range from fear of contamination to religious preoccupation. However, one thing even more common with OCD is the belief by most, if not all, OCD sufferers that they are meant to think in a certain way or have certain thoughts only. Any other pattern of thinking or thoughts is out-rightly condemned as bad, dangerous, and harmful. To understand the nature of OCD and how it develops in the mind, there are some things that you must understand. To begin with, OCD is a process detailed with many steps and each step occurs after the other and this all happens in your head.

Firstly, you have the triggers. These are stimuli, situations, or events that set you off. This may be something like you wanting to leave the house or touching a dirty surface or thinking of sex. It's natural to think of sex, right? But an OCD sufferer conceives in his mind that God may punish him just because he thought of sex.

Once an OCD trigger is set off, random thoughts and images immediately pop up in your head. For instance, if your trigger was a random thought of sex, you may start having thoughts of sex with an animal or a child and then, you'd be like "Why am I having these disgusting and totally sick thoughts?!" Sometimes, these thoughts may be accompanied by an equally disgusting image that represents the thoughts.

Then, what happens next? You begin to evaluate these disgusting thoughts you just had, in a negative light. Remember that this is all happening in your head. You start to think there is definitely something wrong with you and your thinking because you are meant to have pure and good thoughts only; you shouldn't be thinking about pedophilia. A lot of "shoulds" and "shouldn'ts" pop up in your evaluation of how you are to think or feel. Unsurprisingly, you further think that now that these thoughts have appeared in your head, your duty is to suppress, control, or get rid of them. To you, getting rid of the thoughts has become a mission that must be accomplished. You are now the thought police.

Now, you move on to the self-monitoring stage. You constantly watch yourself and your thoughts in a bid to catch those thoughts before they come to your conscious mind. What you don't know however is that the more you try to find that particular thought, the more it appears in your head. Why? Because watching out for the thought means you have to think about it. Thus, you are involuntarily thinking more of this thought by trying to monitor it. At this state, you also have a need for certainty. You want to be sure about whether this thought will make you lose control and act it out.

Then comes the thought-action fusion stage. Here, you start thinking in your mind that having that disgusting thought is the equivalent of committing the action it portrays. For example: you think that thinking of violence means you are going to become violent. Your mind now has a singular interpretation of thoughts, actions, and reality and they are all one. There is absolutely no difference.

Once you start having a fusion of thought and action, you consciously start trying to suppress your thoughts. You do this in the bid to ensure you don't carry out that action. This may work for just about 3 minutes but it is only a temporary retreat; the thoughts come rushing back in no time and it becomes clear that you have no control over them. At this point, you conclude that you have completely lost control. In your opinion, control equates to being able to get rid of unwanted thoughts and since you are unable to do that, it means you have no control over your life or anything else. The more you try to control these thoughts and suppress them, the more you fail and the more you feel out of control.

So then, compulsions set in at this stage. You feel that you have to perform a sort of ritual to neutralize the possibility of you acting your thought out or your thoughts happening. You may choose to wash your hands repeatedly, pray over and over to God so he can keep the evil thoughts away, arrange your things in a certain way, etc. You do these things over and over in a frenetic manner until you feel a sense of absolution. You say, "I can stop doing this now because I feel like I have done enough." Then, this sense of absolution or completion you feel at performing the rituals becomes the new rule you live by. You conclude that you only need to do the rituals until you feel you have done enough. You become hooked on the rituals.

Intriguingly, the mind of an OCD sufferer doesn't stop at this. It goes further to convince you that the next step of action is to start avoiding triggers. "Don't touch the dirty surface; don't think of sex; don't leave the stove on," and on it goes like that. So, you start avoiding shaking people's hands, using public restrooms, seeing people who make you have disgusting sexual feelings. You avoid, avoid, and avoid until you no longer want to see the world.

This exactly is how OCD works in the mind. Before you can understand what steps to take to manage your intrusive thoughts yourself even before seeking professional help, it only makes sense that you would try to understand how your mind works as an individual with OCD first.

CHAPTER FOUR:
THE NATURE OF INTRUSIVE THOUGHTS

As a human being, it is quite normal for you to say "Oh, I just thought about this," or "I thought about that just now." For instance, you could have a thought about something that happened at your workplace early in the day. This is because thoughts are an inherent part of you. Thought may come in the form of ideas, memories, pictures, and images. Usually, they are short and discrete and they don't go on and on in your head unless you consciously choose to replay them in your head. All humans experience thoughts and we all have no issue identifying and sharing our thoughts with others.

From a neuro-scientific perspective, it is not yet certain what thoughts are exactly. Yes, we know that thoughts are the results of brain function, but what we don't know is what exactly about brain function produces thoughts? Is it the work of some neuron or a group of neurons? Do thoughts need some areas of the brain to be activated before they form? Science just doesn't understand that yet.

Not minding where exactly thoughts originate

from, what we do know is that thoughts have to originate in your conscious mind before you regard them as thoughts and there are those that go on in your subconscious mind referred to as automatic thoughts. To understand the basis of intrusive thoughts, you must endeavor to first understand what thoughts are and how thinking works.

According to experts, we think in three possible patterns: logical, pathological, and psychological thinking.

- **Pathological thoughts:** "Pathological thought cannot see itself." Pathological is used to refer to thinking that is dictated by an imbalance in emotion. This doesn't mean the emotion associated is automatically a negative one although this kind of thinking may be influenced by anger or fear, which are the most common form of negative emotions. Pathological thinking is fueled by emotion and it is usually this emotion that drives that thinking.
- **Logical thoughts:** "Logical thought only sees itself." Many people make the mistake of thinking logical thoughts are quite commonplace but this isn't so. Logical thinking isn't as popular as we would probably like it to be. Generally, humans are only able to think logically when faced with

new challenges or difficulty. Logical thoughts are not driven by emotions; they work by a "yes or no" principle i.e. it is either this or it isn't. Logical thinking takes an impartial and objective approach.

- **Psychological thoughts:** "Psychological thoughts see everything." It sees itself and also pathological and logical thoughts. It reflects and aims to self-evaluate. Psychological thoughts try to understand.

While it's hard to say exactly if intrusive thoughts are pathological or psychological because they can't be logical, obviously, one thing we all agree on about intrusive thoughts is that they are mostly unwanted. You don't invite them but they come storming into your head like they own the place or pay rent. One thing you should also know is that these thoughts are more pathological than psychological.

There must have been times when you randomly thought of a lyric from one Beyoncé's songs you don't actually like or a random thought of your first relationship, which went awfully bad, pops up in your head. Somehow, it's always the things that bring negative feelings that play and replay in your head without conscious permission from you.

Intrusive thoughts are thoughts that randomly

enter your consciousness, usually without prompting or caution with alarming, disturbing, and utterly strange content. As we have reiterated right from the first chapter, intrusive thoughts may be unsolicited but we all experience them once in a while. They can range from mildly annoying to out rightly shocking and chaotic. In cases like OCD where these negative thoughts are nowhere near mild, they get stuck and obstruct optimal human functioning. Although there is no identified reason why intrusive thoughts enter the head, researchers and psychologists have tried to come up with different theories to explain this situation.

In 2016, Lynn Somerstein, a psychologist, suggested that recurring intrusive thoughts may be a pointer to something difficult in a person's life. Perhaps the problem could be related to their work, relationship, or something entirely different. However, the main theme of Somerstein's suggestion is that these problems are what pop up in the form of intrusive thoughts. Another psychologist has argued that we actually have these intrusive thoughts because they aren't things we can do. What this means is that while we would actually never consider doing these things we think about in our mind, our brain intentionally coughs them out into our consciousness. But why is this? It probably just feels like it. Other psychologists have posited that the brain just likes to produce junk thoughts which is exactly what intrusive thought are. But, these intrusive thoughts have no meaning until we actually attach meaning to them, based on our feelings or some other reasons. When you don't give meaning to intrusive thoughts, they simply go away from your consciousness.

One question you probably have on your mind like everybody else is: "What controls these negative thoughts and why do they even occur?" Can you even control these unwanted thoughts? Based on evidence provided from researchers, it appears that humans have learned to prevent intrusive thoughts from completely taking over their minds through some designated defensive mechanism put in place. Specifically, this defense mechanism is a neurological control system located in the prefrontal cortex, which is the area of the brain responsible for executive control and the obstruction of intrusive thoughts.

However, this mechanism that we have in place sometimes fails and this is usually what results in cases like obsessive compulsive disorder and a range of other mental disorders. Beyond the power of the prefrontal cortex, researchers have also identified another region of the brain that may be responsible for the inability to prevent intrusive thoughts. This region of the brain is referred to as the hippocampus and based on new evidence, it has been understood that the hippocampus may also be involved in the pathological generation of intrusive thoughts.

GABA, a neurotransmitter recognized for its inhibitory elements, has been directly linked to irregular hippocampal activation and cases of intrusive thoughts. However, researchers have no idea what the mechanisms beneath hippocampal GABA activity in the brain are or whether they have control over unwanted intrusive thoughts. This aims to provide the neural reason for why people with OCD and other related conditions find it impossible to stop and control intrusive thoughts, making them grow stronger and stronger till they dominate the mind and disrupt the person's functionality and health.

An important question you may want to ask is, "why are intrusive thoughts always negative?" Seriously, why can't you have random thoughts of yourself chilling on an island in Santorini? Why do your intrusive thoughts have to be about you hurting yourself or someone else? The best way to understand the reason for this is to understand that intrusive thoughts usually attach themselves to the things that are most important to you. For example, if you are a big fan of dogs, your intrusive thoughts may include disturbing thoughts of you maiming and butchering your cute Frenchie. It is as bad and as simple as that.

Intrusive thoughts often go against your core beliefs and values. Your mind generates about 70,000 thoughts every day but you only pay attention to the most important ones, the ones that appeal to you. Surely, if a thought that goes against your core values enters your head, your mind would immediately pay attention to it and probably say something like "I would never do that!" out loud or to yourself. In essence, what this means is that the values and beliefs you hold play a huge part in determining the thoughts you pay attention to. When an intrusive thought that goes directly against your values pop up in your head, your first reaction would be to generate a feeling of alarm, disgust, or fear. These are all negative emotions and they inadvertently make you believe that the thought may be stronger than it appears.

Therefore, when you wonder about why intrusive thoughts are always about bad and negative things, remember that it varies from person to person because intrusive thoughts appear in the form of what goes against your most important values. Using that example of a dog again: someone else who doesn't think much of dogs may have this same thought and dismiss it immediately because they simply aren't interested enough in dogs to care about killing them. This also explains why OCD symptoms vary from person to person, depending on the sort of OCD subtype they are suffering from.

There are different types of intrusive thoughts that OCD sufferers have to deal with and it may not be the same thought for everybody; in fact, it certainly cannot be. Below, let's check out some of the most common intrusive thoughts OCD sufferers deal with.

The first are **disturbing sexual thoughts**. Note that this isn't to say sexual thoughts are the most common intrusive thoughts in people with OCD, it is simply what we are starting with. Disturbing sexual thoughts may include thoughts of violent sexual activities, sex with inanimate objects, and sex with inappropriate people and figures, and any thought that assumes a sexual nature which you find utterly disturbing and uncomfortable. These kind of thoughts are especially disturbing and distressing when they actually make you aroused. Even when you haven't carried out the act, the mere thought of it gets you aroused, making you feel even more ashamed and scared. This, however, doesn't mean you would really do it or the thought is your reality; that is just your body giving a normal physiological response. Most people tend to come to an erroneous conclusion that the thought must be true since they experienced arousal.

Another type of intrusive thoughts is the one **involving kids.** These types of thoughts are very disturbing specifically because they may contain content of you harming a child or children in whatever way. You may think of yourself harming your own child, something you could never do. Intrusive thoughts also come in the form of **aggressive acts towards others.** They usually involve thoughts of you causing harm to other people and sometimes, yourself. Again, these thoughts cause distress especially when you are the type who would never even hurt a fly. It often comes with an impulse to aggressively attack someone physically or verbally.

Certain intrusive thoughts also take the form of **disturbing religious thoughts.** You may have inappropriate sexual thoughts of religious figures, think of yourself cursing and swearing during worship or prayer or, have a strong impulse to do something inappropriate during religious services or events. Although it is certainly normal and okay to have these kind of thoughts ambush your consciousness once in a long while, many people find it difficult to shake these thoughts off and they are often considered dangerous, irresponsible, and harmful. There is a tendency for most people to consider the possibility of something being wrong with them when they have these thoughts. Some may even consider the possibility of themselves having these thoughts because they have probably done something related, but they really are just normal thoughts that other people also have occasionally.

A particularly interesting type of intrusive thought is the one that drives the homosexual OCD. These are intrusive thoughts that make you question your sexual identity and orientation. This isn't about people who already know that they are attracted to people of the same sex, but rather about heterosexual people who keep having intrusive thoughts that make them wonder if they are really straight. These people are usually still heterosexual but these thoughts prompt them to start doubting their sexuality.

Some people experience intrusive thoughts about death; they constantly worry about the possibility of death and also imagine giving up the ghost at any given time. Sometimes, these thoughts may not be about them but about someone close to them. There are times when intrusive thoughts are simply about your safety and the safety of the people dearest to you. Of course, it is normal to worry about your family and friends when they are apart from you but sometimes, the worrying becomes too excessive to the point where you may have disturbing images of someone in danger inside in your head. For example, you may think they have been in an accident or something really bad has happened to them. These kinds of thoughts compel you to ensure they are really safe. You might find yourself calling them repeatedly just to be assured of their safety and this may even get to a point where they become annoyed or irritated. In cases like this, these intrusive thoughts only stop when you see them arrive safely at home. If you have these kind of intrusive thoughts, it may prompt you to take some drastic measures to ensure your loved ones come to no harm. For instance, you may irrationally limit your kids' activities to the indoors so as to reduce the possibility of them getting into an accident.

Intrusive thoughts are completely normal but how you interpret and react to them is what determines whether they have a negative impact on your life or not. If you have an intrusive thought of you harming someone but you pay no mind to it, your mind would move on from the thought in no time. But, if you have this thought and you start creating a narrative around it, it would become the focus of your mind until it leads to a compulsive behavior. The one difference between normal intrusive thoughts and distressing intrusive thoughts is the response you give to each.

WHAT IS THE DIFFERENCE BETWEEN INTRUSIVE THOUGHTS AND URGES?

Regarding obsessive compulsive disorder, two things you will hear over and over are: urges and intrusive thoughts. However, are they the same? In a way, your urges and intrusive thoughts are the same; they both make up what is known as obsession. Both may be regarded as symptoms of obsessions when it comes to OCD. However, an intrusive thought isn't really an obsession until you respond to it in a certain way and it makes you feel like performing a compulsive behavior.

Urges come from intrusive thoughts. If you have a thought about kissing someone, that's not an urge. It becomes an urge when you actually feel like carrying the thought out. In OCD cases, urges are usually there to make you do something that won't let your thoughts come to pass. If you have the thought that you could harm someone, then you get an urge to get rid of everything you could possibly use in harming this person. Let's say you get an intrusive thought that you have done something really bad and you are an evil person; you may have an urge to confess the bad thing you think you did so people would recognize you for what you think you really are.

There are many myths surrounding unwanted intrusive thoughts. One of these is the belief that having unwanted intrusive thoughts means that you have a subconscious fantasy to carry out these thoughts that come to your mind but this is just what it is, a myth. In fact, it's clearly the opposite. It is that effort you put in to ensure you don't really act out the thought that makes you get stuck in the loop of that thought. Another myth many people belief about intrusive thoughts is that they may be some sort of message and they need to be examined more closely. In truth though, they are not messages or warnings despite how they make you feel. They are simply thoughts. Most people make the mistake of considering these intrusive thoughts and impulses as the same thing.

CHAPTER FIVE:
HOW INTRUSIVE THOUGHTS LEAD TO COMPULSIVE BEHAVIORS

It is quite difficult to understand how some mere thoughts can drive a person to indulge in seemingly ridiculous and nonsensical behavior repeatedly – when you are looking at it from the perspective of a loved one or someone without OCD. People with OCD however understand the absolute fear and emotion that come from having these thoughts. To make sense of the whole compulsion thing, you have to first make sense of how OCD is even maintained in the first place. Many people probably feel like, "why can't you just perform the compulsion once and be done? Why does it have to be done repeatedly?" Well, this is obviously a good question that we have to examine in depth. The two main things to understand here are: how intrusive thoughts cause distress and the things that keep the thoughts and compulsive behaviors going. In essence, you must try to understand how intrusive thoughts drive and maintain compulsions.

Before we go ahead, it is absolutely important for you to understand that each person's OCD experience is unique, diverse, and complex. There absolutely cannot be one answer for every individual; it is the job of your professional therapist to help you seek your individual answer, specific to you. What you are about to learn from this chapter is simply how intrusive thoughts keep OCD going.

The first place to start is to identify the two beliefs that are common with most, if not all people with OCD. These are:

- An inflated sense of responsibility: OCD sufferers believe they have a responsibility for keeping themselves, their loved ones, and other people around from harm or danger.
- Over-exaggeration of threat: They also have a belief that their thoughts contain more risk than they do.

Even though you have probably heard this before, people with OCD are usually of the belief that what happens in their intrusive thoughts are very likely to happen in reality and so, they have a responsibility to ensure it never does; therefore, they must take actions to prevent it. These two beliefs (which are cognitive by the way) are responsible for that continuous cycle of obsessions and compulsive behaviors which people with OCD often find themselves in. Even when the OCD sufferer knows that an intrusive thought have relatively low levels of risk, the heightened sense of responsibility is what often directs them to engage in compulsive behaviors. This also explains why professionals have suggested that only mostly people with good values suffer from OCD. Have you ever seen a morally bankrupt person with a sense of responsibility anyway?

Intrusive thoughts result in negative emotions, particularly fear, and this further drives compulsive behaviors. People who suffer from obsessive compulsive disorder are driven by a fear of consequences, no matter how unlikely these consequences seem. There is always an exaggerated perception of risk involved. A 0.01% risk may seem like 99.9 to someone with OCD.

Cognition affects emotions and emotions also affect cognition. In this regard, the kind of emotions generated by the intrusion of a disturbing thought plays a part in how an individual gets stuck in the obsessions-compulsions cycle. As someone with OCD, how you respond emotionally to intrusive thoughts explains the origin of your emotions. Cognition, emotion, and affect all have a relationship that makes them affect one another in a sense. The emotional response you give to your thoughts will always determine how you act or behave, whether you are an OCD sufferer or not. For example: if you have a thought about harming someone you are actually close with at school, the likely emotional response you give would be that of horror or even guilt (for having such a thought). When you see this person at school the next day, you may behave guiltily by not being able to look them in the eyes when having a conversation. On the contrary, if the thought was about someone you actually consider cruel or evil, the likely emotional response from you may be that of amusement or indifference. When you see this person the next day at school, your behavior towards them may take on a snide approach because you would probably be like, "If only you know what I do to you in my head, you evil person." How the thought makes you feel all depends on the context, situation, and your belief.

Looking at another example: let's say you are fast asleep and you suddenly heard some noise down your stairs. There are three possible reactions:

- Firstly, you could think that was just your dog downstairs again (think), turn your nose in slight annoyance (feel) and simply go back to bed (act).

- Secondly, you could think (thought), 'oh, that's my boyfriend coming in, I better go welcome him,' stand up enthusiastically (feel) and hurry down to say hello (act).
- Thirdly, you could think that is a thief downstairs (thought), become frightened and anxious (feel), and then proceed to call the police (act).

From this example, the event is all the same but the emotional responses and behaviors are different. What this portrays is that the same situation can make people have completely different emotional reactions and then shape the way they behave, based on the belief they have about the event and the context of the event itself.

Intrusive thoughts cause some people to act in certain ways even when they know they are potentially at no risk. OCD is the result of the mind conceiving perceived risks and pushing people to do something to prevent the perceived risks out of your sense of responsibility. Individuals with OCD believe that they have to do something in the eventuality of their thought coming to pass, even when they know they are being extremely cautious. "I just have to wash my hands. Who knows if this extremely white and sparkly surface has some hidden germs even though it looks clean?"

Intrusive thoughts have huge powers, enough to make people engage in seemingly ridiculous compulsions due to the fact that they elicit negative feelings, mostly of fear and anxiety. For someone who doesn't know what it feels like to have OCD, it may be difficult to see how a fleeting, insignificant thought can influence a person to the point where they have to engage in some rituals. It's also quite difficult to explain but what you should know about OCD is that it is a sort of anxiety disorder and the feelings of fear that come with intrusive thoughts often leave an OCD sufferer in a prolonged state of anxiety which literally heightens the level of anxiety. If you have ever been anxious for a long period of time, then you would agree that it doesn't feel nice, comfortable or fun in any way. Now imagine being in a constant state of anxiety because this is exactly what OCD feels like.

Anxiety is a natural emotion that is used to help us sense and avoid danger or potentially dangerous situations. For instance, if you go for a walk at night (on a lonely road) with your earpiece plugged in your ears while you are listening to music and then you suddenly feel someone walking behind you, immediately, your senses become heightened, your heart starts racing and your muscles stiffen. These are physiological reactions pointing to anxiety, caused by your perception of potential danger. So, you start to walk faster and you do so until you appear on a busier road or you get home. In this situation, the feeling of fear and anxiety were what alerted you to possible harm from the person walking behind you. Since the anxiety was to shield you from danger, it reduces the nearer you get to your home or the busier road and immediately subsides once you get home. Your anxiety drops to the normal level, you blame yourself for walking alone on the lonely road on a super dark night with no light of the moon and soon, your anxiety is completely evaporated.

This is a normal response everybody gives to an anxious situation; it is called the "fight or flight" response. It is your body's way of alerting you to danger. Once the danger has passed, your anxiety also subsides. For people with OCD however, the anxiety never goes; it remains there because the thought of perceived harm or danger is also there, lurking in the mind and snapping at the consciousness at will. Anxiety levels remain high due to the perception of risk and the huge sense of responsibility OCD sufferers feel for preventing the bad thought from happening and also because of the unwanted intrusive thoughts which further highlight and magnify the perceived risk. These thoughts, perpetual state of anxiety, and the sense of responsibility compel the person to do something that would help prevent such thing for happening. That is how compulsive behaviors begin until they become a cycle with obsession.

When a person continues to perform or act out compulsions, it becomes difficult for them to learn that what they fear wouldn't have happened whether they did the compulsion or not. It also means that they can't find out that there is actually no reason to further engage in the compulsive behavior. This cycle becomes vicious, with the recurring obsessional thoughts, compulsions, and the state of anxiety that never diminishes. Therefore, for individuals with OCD, anxiety-inducing thoughts lead to negative interpretation of the context and content of those thoughts. This is why even when nothing happens, the heightened state of anxiety remains until the person performs the compulsion. In time, this person may even come to believe that the reason nothing bad hasn't happened is because they have been performing the compulsions, making it even harder to stop compulsive behavior. Since the negative interpretations of the intrusive thoughts never go away anyway, these thoughts continue to facilitate a need for safety seeking behaviors. So, in a bid to get themselves out of a ditch, people with OCD sink even further.

Doubt is another reason why people with OCD engage in compulsive behaviors and never stop. Remember that a French psychiatrist once referred to OCD as the "madness of doubt." The level of anxiety in an OCD sufferer is usually proportionate to the level of perceived risk or danger. The worse the level of danger perceived, the higher the fear of something bad happening and the more compelled a person feels to do something to prevent the risk. And here is how doubt comes to play in the OCD situation. OCD has an intolerability for uncertainty so it demands yes or no answers; it is either black or it is white, nothing like grey when it comes to this.

Another feeling many people tend to ignore when talking about OCD and related conditions is that feeling of guilt. While fear will always play a part, it seems like guilt is the main feeling behind OCD in some people. Naturally, no one likes to feel guilty, especially when it is over something they didn't even do. However, when you have a nagging thought of causing harm to others, it may result in feelings of guilt, which becomes pathological when it gets too intense and severe.

A new theory, which is pretty interesting, has suggested that in some cases, hypersensitivity to the emotion of guilt may result in the development and maintenance of OCD in certain people. In fact, if you are someone who is extremely sensitive to guilt, then you are very prone to developing and maintaining obsessive compulsive disorder. In context, the emotion can either be that of guilt or an irrational fear of guilt. Apparently, you can be pretty scared of guilt and lead yourself down the road to developing obsessions and compulsions.

According to a new study published in *Clinical Psychology and Psychotherapy*, people with OCD may have a more threatening perception of guilt than normal people and people without OCD do, making guilt unbearable and intolerable for them. Instead of the normal feeling of fear, any unwanted intrusive thought which inspires guilty feelings may be countered with extreme anxiety and a compulsive need to get rid of the mental intrusion. Several researches have been conducted with findings that suggest that being vulnerable to guilt makes you prone to developing OCD. However, this new study suggests that OCD is not developed simply by being prone to guilt, but rather by an extreme sensitivity to guilt.

In other words, OCD isn't driven by guilt itself but by a fear of guilt. To make it clearer, OCD sufferers don't perform compulsive behaviors to avoid intrusive thoughts. Rather, they perform compulsions to avoid feeling guilty in the future due to their fear of having that kind of emotion. They just don't like to feel guilty so they try to avoid things that would make them feel guilty. In a way, it still boils down to guilt though. In these cases, compulsions are motivated by a need to avoid this emotion and not just to prevent the thought from happening. As an example: let's say you have a violently intrusive thought about dropping a baby down the stairs. If you are the type who is sensitive to guilt, this thought may make you feel guilty despite not having performed the action. "Oh, why would I even think of dropping a baby in the first place? That is just so cruel and inhumane." So, you feel guilty for having the thought. To avoid that feeling of guilt in future, you start fighting and suppressing the thought so it doesn't just barge into your head uninvited again. To further combat the thought, you may start engaging in covert or mental compulsions to keep the thought away. For instance, saying "I can't drop a baby" repeatedly may be you way of carrying out a mental compulsion that helps keep the thought away and ultimately helps you prevent the possibility of experiencing that feeling of guilt again. The lead doctor of this study concludes that fear of guilt is central to OCD just like fear of fear is central to panic disorders.

As long as doubt remains, obsessions will continue to result in compulsive behaviors. However, once a person learns to accept that doubt and uncertainty are a constant part of life and he or she learns to live with them, breaking free from the shackles of obsessional thoughts and compulsive behaviors become much easier. This brings us to acceptance as the first strategic approach to breaking free from intrusive thoughts and OCD.

CHAPTER SIX:
ACCEPTANCE: THE FIRST STEP TO OVERCOMING INTRUSIVE THOUGHTS AND COMPULSIVE BEHAVIORS

The one thing people with OCD often think of is "change." How can compulsive behaviors be changed? "How do I change my obsessional thinking pattern?" Change is a constant part of life; we all have to undergo some changes at different points in our lives. In most OCD treatment, mental health professionals also emphasize the need for change. However, when the talk and thinking about change becomes too much, it is quite easy to trivialize something which is just as important as change in the treatment of OCD conditions, maybe even more important. Without this thing, change would never and could never happen. What is this thing? Acceptance.

The first step to changing your OCD is to accepting it. Acceptance means to come into agreement with something, believe in it, and regard it as the truth or reality. Acceptance of something doesn't necessarily mean you like it or you have accepted defeat; it simply means you are being objective enough to recognize that this thing really does exist and it is affecting you. Several things exist that we do not like, but we have no choice but to accept their reality. Your obsessive compulsive disorder condition is one of those things.

Many people with OCD cannot tolerate the idea of acknowledging or accepting the fact that they are suffering from this condition and it is really affecting their lives in different negative ways. For these people, it doesn't matter whether they go for treatment therapy or not, they find that they are unable to change much of their thinking or behaviors. Most times, they are simply unable to follow through with the treatment process. "I'm not even sure I need this therapy. It's not as bad as it seems." As a wise person once said though, you cannot change a thing unless you accept that thing." Therefore, you cannot change your OCD unless you accept that it exists and is your reality, no matter how painful that is.

It would not be fallacy to say that the mental-health field is obsessed with the idea of change. Professionals want to do everything they can to change people's disorders or conditions and that is really admirable. However, there are a whole lot of things that can't be changed no matter how hard you try. In truth, the main thing that mental health professionals should start with is teaching patients to accept themselves. If you have OCD, then you should accept that you have OCD. Do not try to sugarcoat it or give it a name that makes you feel more comfortable. Do not act like it isn't having a negative impact on your quality of living. Even when you go for OCD treatment, you may not be able to get rid of your symptoms a hundred percent. So, accepting this right from the start makes it easier for you to work on your OCD.

Before you can start working towards changing your OCD, you must first accept a number of facts, including:

- You are suffering from OCD.
- Your OCD is chronic.
- There is no one to make you better other than yourself.
- Your OCD isn't a choice.
- You need patience and hard work to start getting better.
- To really confront and change your condition, you would have to experience anxiety and discomfort a lot of times.
- The path to recovery isn't always smooth.
- You would have to work hard every single day, just to keep your OCD symptoms away...

- Even when you are already recovering, there may slips of symptoms. This won't affect your recovery.
- Whatever part of your life you have lost to the disorder, you may not get it back in full again.

When you are unable to accept any or all of the above facts, what accompanies the lack of acceptance is some negative emotional response like anger, anxiety, or depression. These emotional responses will create the exact opposite of what you want. The anger you feel from not being able to accept the reality could create distress that further worsens your OCD symptoms.

This is why it is important for you to accept the fact that change and acceptance are two mutually inclusive concepts; they aren't exclusive of each other. Actually acceptance is one of the most effective ways of initiating change, if not the most effective. The biggest obstruction OCD sufferers have is the illogical strategies they employ in their bid to cope with their obsessional thoughts and that is what you know as compulsions.

Compulsions only give temporary relief to anxiety. The more you engage in compulsive behaviors, the more it becomes a habit and in no time, it becomes the problem you have to contend with. As a strategic approach to treat OCD, acceptance means letting go of that struggle to fight your obsessions via compulsions. It also means turning to more effective solutions, such as cognitive behavioral therapy. So, how do you adopt acceptance?

The first step to acceptance is to understand that things cannot always be the way you want it to be in life. They can only be the way they are. Humans are wishful creatures, and although there is really nothing wrong with wishing, it is also important that we as humans accept the fact that we don't have the power to make some things be as we want them to be. As a person with OCD, it is especially difficult to resist making such demands, especially since it is harder to control your life and what happens to you. Always keep it in mind that acceptance isn't liking something; it is simply seeing it as the reality. You aren't accepting your OCD because you like it; you are accepting it because you understand the fact that it is your reality.

Another thing you must do to practice acceptance is to live in the moment and avoid projecting yourself into the future. Living in the present means neither looking at the past nor being worried about the future. Some OCD sufferers obsess over the past, thinking about what has happened and what might have happened if they had done this and not done that. No matter how hard you try, you can't change the past. Avoid using "what ifs" to live in the future. People with OCD spend a lot of time trying to predict or control the future in order to prevent harm from coming to them or other people. They fail to realize that this is a fruitless endeavor because no one can ever predict the future or have a solution to every potential outcome.

The only reasonable thing to do is to concentrate on the moment and live in the present. Do your best to immerse yourself in whatever you wish to achieve at any moment in time. Don't bother about what may happen in the future or how this may pan out. The idea behind this is for you to eliminate all other considerations and direct your mental and physical energies towards accomplishing the goals you have at hand. If you think you can't possibly achieve this, think of all the times when you were combatting your obsessions by devoting all your energy to performing compulsions so they can go away. In a way, you were already working towards achieving a goal, but you were doing this in a negative rather than positive way.

Also, it is crucial that you have an understanding of what exactly you are accepting. There are 5 important things you must bring yourself to accept in the path to eliminating intrusive obsessional thoughts and compulsive behaviors:

- Self-acceptance: Accept yourself unconditionally as a human who isn't perfect and can make mistakes. Understand the fact that you should never judge yourself based on a few symptoms or characteristics.
- Acceptance of others: Understand that just like you, other people are imperfect too. The fact that they don't have OCD like you doesn't change this reality. Understand that they don't have to support you in your path to recovery if they don't want to.
- Acceptance of your OCD: Understand that it is what it is and you can't change this. OCD is chronic and the fact that you have it doesn't mean you have an unfair life. More importantly, accept the fact that it is possible for you to recover as long as you work hard at it.
- Accept that you need therapy: You should understand that nobody can facilitate your recovery except you. Your therapy requires hard work, diligence, and could bring discomfort but you should be ready to put the effort in.

- Acceptance of the process of recovery: Understand that recovery is an active process and an on-going one at that. However, this process isn't a smooth one. Accept the fact that there will be slips and lapses along the path but this doesn't change anything. It only means you are working hard and creating a better life for yourself.

Looking at all these things, your goal may seem difficult or impossible to achieve, but the truth is it is achievable if you put your mind to it. Learn to persevere no matter the process. Ensure that you don't quit your efforts even as you work on the acceptance and get started on your path to recovery. After acceptance, the next path to recovery is to get rid of intrusive thoughts so you can stop the compulsive behaviors.

CHAPTER SEVEN:
OVERCOMING INTRUSIVE THOUGHTS FOR LIFE

The thought-action fusion process is one of the reasons why intrusive thoughts seem too overwhelming for OCD sufferers to overcome. Individuals with OCD often believe that thinking about something disturbing is the equivalent of carrying out the act. Someone with OCD is of the belief that simply thinking about a car accident could make the accident happen. Due to this, OCD sufferers try to monitor dangerous thoughts so they can suppress them. For some people with OCD, there is nothing like thought-action fusion, they simply have to deal with obsessional thoughts. Suppressing or monitoring intrusive thoughts isn't the way to overcoming their invasion into your mind, so what is?

The first thing you should know is that you should never try to stop or suppress intrusive thoughts. Although it may appear easier to say than to believe, the thing is your thoughts are words and ideas that pop uninvited into your mind; they pose no potential danger. You don't have to take these thoughts seriously just because they are in your head. As a person with OCD, you should understand that your thoughts aren't a representation of your values or your morals. In fact, OCD intrusive thoughts are usually a reflection of the very things you find offensive as an individual, things that go against your values and morals. Despite how hard it may be, you should never try to push intrusive thoughts away because this just makes them come back even more and leads you to a point of obsession.

Instead, what you should do is let these thoughts flow freely as they come. Make an effort not to be upset over the thoughts; accept that they are real but don't try to analyze or dissect them too much. The idea is not to focus your strength on fighting the intrusive thoughts but to change the emotional responses to the intrusive thoughts you have. Make a decision to assume an objective point of view to your intrusive thoughts; assume a non-judgmental stance and accept the thoughts as they come. Let the thought remain for as long as it wishes. Eventually, it will pass and come back again. But, that's all right because it will go back again.

Once you learn to stop holding the thoughts back or trying to suppress them, you should also learn to stop shaming yourself or feeling guilty for having the thoughts. Stop giving the emotional response that makes the intrusive thoughts feel satisfied that they have achieved their aims. These thoughts are normal and that is why you can't change them. But, what you can change is the emotional response you give to them and how you interpret them. Another important thing in your path to overcoming intrusive thoughts is to see intrusive thoughts for what they really are. Immediately you stop fighting intrusive thoughts, then you open yourself to seeing these thoughts in a new light. At this point, you can embrace the obsessive thoughts for what they are.

One absolutely important approach to stopping or reducing intrusive thoughts in OCD is to identify the opposite value of these thoughts. Usually, every intrusive thought that you experience has an opposite value which you can use to generate an opposing thought that combats obsessional thinking. Let's assume that you have obsessive thoughts about committing violent acts. The very fact that this is the kind of intrusive thought you have and the fact that it makes you feel distressed means that your values and morals go against the commiting violence. If you were a violent person by nature, then you wouldn't find violent thoughts to be distressing or uncomfortable; they would just be mere thoughts to you. So, the point here is to counter the intrusive thoughts by creating your own thoughts, which are the direct opposite of your violent thoughts.

For example: if you have a thought like "I am going to stab my roommate to death with a knife," counter it with an opposite thought that goes like "I am a good person. I am going to help my roommate with his project tomorrow." Just think of something that aligns with your values as a person. The interesting thing about your mind is that despite generating thousands of thoughts every day, it can only occupy one thought at a time. You can't think of two things at a time. Of course, it may seem like there are plenty of thoughts swimming around in your head at any given moment but you can only think one thought at a time. Therefore, when you immediately counter an intrusive thought with an opposite thought, this intrusive thought immediately goes away. If it keeps coming back, keep countering it with a positive thought until it reclines away from your mind. It may not be easy doing this but the more you practice, the easier it gets.

OCD can be likened to a fear network in your brain,

alerting you when there is any sign of danger so you can do something immediately. Obsessive thoughts only occur surrounding the most feared consequences to you. If you do not have a fear of something, then related scenarios wouldn't come as an intrusive thought to you. You care deeply about your family and that is why you probably have thoughts of "If I don't check the stove to make sure it's off, the house will burn and my family will all be dead." This is a scare tactic OCD uses to muddle up your mind. Once you recognize the fact that it's just a scare tactic, you can learn to counter this tactic easily so it doesn't have any effect on you. The more you react to the intrusive thoughts with fear, the more you experience them.

As you have already learned in an early chapter, one of the most effective methods for combatting intrusive thoughts and OCD as a whole is the Exposure and Response Prevention (ERP) treatment. With OCD, you don't have a way past it; you only get a way through it. As you already know, the more you avoid intrusive thoughts, the more you experience them and the more distress they bring. So, the next step of action to overcoming intrusive thoughts is to practice going head-to-head with that thought while disengaging from the urge to perform any compulsion meant to give temporary relief from distress. Usually, compulsions are meant to give you the assurance you need to believe that you won't really carry out your thought or you are not what your thought portrays. The ideal way to go about ERP is to organize exposure tasks hierarchically; make the steps gradual and slight so that you can slowly let your intrusive thoughts and OCD know that there is nobody else in charge but you. We will of course more talk about this method of therapy and its many benefits to you.

Finally, it is always nice and it does help to have some support while you try to overcome intrusive thoughts. But, make sure you are seeking your support from the right people and not those who wouldn't be patient enough to see things from your perspective. It is almost impossible to try to conquer OCD on your own even if you are pretty determined. The reason why you need a support structure is because nothing is more powerful in overcoming OCD than an empathetic, compassionate, and informed person to whom you can voice those thoughts you are so scared of. When said out loud to someone understanding, the same unwanted thoughts that make your heart shake in fear will disintegrate immediately and lose their power over you. When you spend time discussing and talking about these thoughts with someone who is capable of still listening to you and not thinking you are crazy for having these thoughts, you find yourself coming to accept the reality of these thoughts being just thoughts. In any case, while it makes sense to have a supportive relative or friend, the ideal person to discuss your case with is a trained and supportive OCD coach with whom you can unravel OCD and see it for what it truly is.

CHAPTER EIGHT:
STAYING CONSCIOUS OF YOUR THOUGHTS WITH MINDFULNESS MEDITATION

In recent years, mindfulness has become a very popular meditation among people trying to switch their thoughts, feelings, and acts from negative to positive. You may have fleetingly heard about mindfulness; it is the ability to remain present in the moment. And, since we already said that the key to ridding yourself of unwanted intrusive thoughts is to neither think about past events nor worry about future ones- just live in the moment, doesn't it make sense that mindfulness would make an ideal strategy for fighting against intrusive and obsessional thoughts in OCD?

Using very simple language, mindfulness can be described as the act of grounding yourself in present moments without any form of judgment. It is an act of self-awareness and self-acceptance. Being mindful means that you are aware of what is going on within and around you, but you accept everything nevertheless. When paired with cognitive behavioral therapy or exposure response prevention therapy, mindfulness can be especially beneficial for people suffering from OCD.

Due to the focus on awareness and acceptance, mindfulness serves as a very efficient technique for diminishing anxiety to the barest minimum. According to mindfulness practice, when you have an intrusive thought pop up in your head, you learn to let the thought remain in your mind while providing it with zero attention or weight. You let yourself experience the thought without trying to suppress it, judge it, change it, or chase it from your mind. You let it pass away on its own without worrying about whether it should be there or not.

Sufficient evidence, in fact, exists to prove the effectiveness of mindfulness meditation in improving the symptoms of obsessive compulsive disorder and other anxiety-induced disorders. Therefore, it makes sense that any form of meditation that embodies the practice of mindfulness would actually play a huge part in the treatment of OCD symptoms. Unfortunately, many OCD sufferers seem to have a preconceived notion that meditation is hard and so harbor a negative disposition towards its practice. They somehow believe that meditation practice is harder for people with OCD and some therapists even encourage this belief.

Mindfulness meditation is one of the easiest meditation techniques because it is already an inherent trait in us. As human beings, we have the innate ability to ground ourselves in the moment without thinking of past events or worrying about the uncertainties the future may hold; we simply need to learn how to harness it, which is exactly what you do when you practice mindfulness meditation. Mindfulness is a quality of being fully engaged with yourself, your thoughts, and your actions in the moment, without being distracted or getting caught up in the thoughts. In training your mind to be present in the moment, you are also training yourselves to live life more mindfully.

One difference exists between mindfulness and other meditation practices, which is why it is easier for people with various challenges to employ it as strategy. Unlike normal meditation, mindfulness isn't a transient state of mind that is only there when you are meditating; it is a way of living that you can incorporate into your life to make it better. Also, mindfulness doesn't get rid of stress, anxiety, and other challenges you are faced with from having OCD; rather, it enables you to become aware of your uncomfortable thoughts and the feelings that arise from these thoughts so your eyes and mind can be opened to how best to handle both. Mindfulness makes it easy for you to take a calm, logical, and rational approach to intrusive thoughts so that you don't have to engage in compulsive behaviors. Of course, practicing mindfulness doesn't mean you would no longer have the intrusive thoughts, it just means that you would become more rational and thoughtful in how you interpret these thoughts and the feelings they bring with them.

Based on science-backed evidence, mindfulness has been proven to have the capacity to change the shape of your brain so you can be geared towards more positive thoughts and emotions. However, mindful meditation doesn't just change the shape of the brain, it can also changes your mindset and perspective so that you improve how you interpret the contents and context of unwanted intrusive thoughts. This should go a long way in helping you understand the hype around mindfulness and why it has become a popular trend.

HOW TO PRACTICE MINDFULNESS
There are many techniques or approaches to practicing mindfulness; the key is to ensure that whatever technique you choose is helping you achieve that state of alertness and awareness you

seek. Any technique you use should also help you achieve focused relaxation, devoid of judgment or sentiments.

There is the basic mindfulness meditation where you simply sit in a quiet space and concentrate on your breathing until you feel like you have done enough. Another technique of mindfulness is the "body sensations" technique where you devote attention to every bodily sensation you have, no matter how subtle; you have to focus on each part of your body in succession.

Sensory is also an approach to mindfulness practice; it involves taking note of all five senses: sights, sounds, tastes, smells, and touches. Emotions is a mindfulness technique where you let everything you are feeling come to the surface without judging or disregarding anything; you simply accept the presence of the feelings and then let go of these emotions. Finally, an effective mindfulness technique for coping with addictive behaviors is 'urge surfing.' It involves teaching yourself to cope with the cravings for whatever substance or behavior you are addicted to and letting it pass.

Here is how to practice the basic mindfulness meditation:

➢ Find a comfortable seat in a quiet and solemn space, devoid of noise or distraction. You can sit on a chair, a cushion, a meditation mat, or the floor depending on your choice. Ensure you are sitting in a relaxed position, with your back straight. Let your feet touch the ground and place your hand directly on your thighs or legs, depending on where you are sitting.

➢ Gently breathe. Notice the rise and fall of your chest as you breathe in and out. Notice the sensation that comes with breathing and also focus on the air, going in and out of your nostrils. Notice the pause you give before each in-breath.

➢ Continue to breathe as you become aware of every sound, sensation, and idea.

➢ Embrace each thought as it comes without labeling it good or bad. Simply label it as "thinking." Return your focus to breathing, even as you catch your mind wandering away.

You can start practicing for just a few minutes each day, but as you improve and make progress, increase the length of your sessions. Just ensure that you practice every day. As you can see, it is quite an easy process so it shouldn't be hard to incorporate it into your daily routine. Once you become good at it, you can even start practicing while you are doing anything or any task. Mindfulness requires about 5 to 10 minutes of practice every day, depending on your choice. Also note that it is best practiced when you are waking and getting up from bed or just going to sleep.

Before you conclude whether mindfulness is really necessary or not, here are 5 tips to help you better understand how to utilize mindfulness to the max:

- Most people make the mistake of thinking the way to practice mindfulness is to focus on the breath only. Yes, concentrating on your breath is a core part of practicing mindfulness but it's not meant to be a static act. Instead of putting all your effort into sticking with your breath, mindfulness is the most effective when you focus gently on the breath. While this means that your attentions will often stray, it also means one more thing for you to be aware of. In trying hard to concentrate on the breath only, many people end up losing touch of the thoughts and sensations they are meant to place focus on and be aware of. The purpose of mindfulness it to help you improve your self-awareness and the ability to notice when you stray from your breath so you can easily return attention back to your breathing. When you notice your attention stray from your breathing, simply acknowledge this and go back to concentrating on your breath. Don't end up prying yourself into the hands of your breath in the bid to let your obsessive thoughts flow freely.

- Another tip to help you more with your mindfulness meditation practice is to know that thinking is allowed. Nothing can stop the conscious mind from generating thousands of thoughts like it does, not even meditation. Most people erroneously assume that you have failed at meditating when you let yourself think but this isn't true. In fact, thinking is a mental activity that should always be part of the meditation process. Recognizing that thinking is a fundamental part of meditation is crucial. What would there be to be mindful of if you couldn't think while meditating anyway? The only thing that shouldn't be a part of your meditation process is mindless and purposeless thinking. Then, you should also never allow yourself to be carried away in your train of thoughts nor should you judge yourself for thinking. Instead, acknowledge and accept the fact that thinking is happening while you are meditating and go back to focusing on your breath.

- People with OCD generally find the thought of being alone with their obsessive thoughts to be really terrifying. The very idea that they need to sit and let their thoughts come and go while they observe can be very scary and uncomfortable for an OCD sufferer. This is because their thoughts taunt, terrify, and terrorize them. For example, if you as an OCD sufferer are practicing mindfulness and concentrating on your breath, then you experience a sudden intrusive thought of your loved one being stabbed with a knife, you may be forced to stop concentrating on your breath and focus on fighting that thought off. In moments like this, what you need to know is that intrusive thoughts will jealously try to get your attention when they notice you aren't really giving it to them. Remember that they are just thoughts and you have the power to simply acknowledge them and return to your mindfulness practice.

- Another popular misconception among OCD sufferers who have tried to use mindfulness in the past is the belief that mindfulness practice is supposed to be anxiety free. They have expectations that there shouldn't be feelings of anxiety when meditating; that the whole point of meditation is defeated when you are anxious while at it. On the contrary, anxiety is an emotion so it only makes sense that it would be a part of the meditation process. In fact, anxiety is just another thing to devote your attention to and be mindful with. The whole idea of meditating is to notice when your attention is concentrated on your anxiety and then return to your breathing. If you spend the whole meditation process going back and forth between the presence of anxiety and your breath, then you have successfully practiced and improved your mindfulness skills.

- The final tip is to never consider your meditation process as an evaluation of your success in the fight against OCD. Many people make the mistake of doing this and it often affects their performance overall. Mindfulness isn't something to succeed in or fail at; it is simply something to improve on. The thing about mindfulness is that you have successfully practiced being mindful even by attempting to be mindful; you don't have to achieve that state of mindfulness. The more you practice, the better your mindfulness skills become and soon, you would be able to achieve that overall sense of mindfulness.

Learn to approach mindfulness practice from a

gentle and realistic perspective, without false expectations or assumptions. This gives you a sense of power that you would definitely require when it comes to cognitive behavioral therapy and exposure response prevention therapy.

Mindfulness has so many benefits to your physical and mental health whether you realize it or not. Practicing mindfulness goes beyond just fighting OCD and becoming self-aware, it can actually help in a lot of ways that could positively impact the quality of your life. All of these benefits of mindfulness that we will be checking out are fully backed by science. Science has actually established that the many benefits of mindfulness meditation can be described as being phenomenal. Mindfulness improves physical, psychological, and emotional health and also facilitates positive changes in thinking, attitude, and behaviors – but that's not all. Let's find out what the more amazing benefits of mindfulness are.

1. MINDFULNESS REDUCES RUMINATION

Undoubtedly, this is one of the things that worsen symptoms of OCD, but with mindfulness, research has shown that you can reduce rumination. Practicing mindfulness decreases rumination and the negative effect it has on your thinking pattern and behaviors. With less rumination, it means you experience less anxiety or depression.

2. IT IMPROVES MENTAL AND PHYSICAL WELLBEING

When you improve your mindfulness skill, you are opening yourself up to a more satisfactory life than the one you already have. Being mindful improves your wellbeing in the sense that you are able to savor the pleasure in situations as you become engaged in activities that interest you. You also develop a strong capacity for dealing with negative and challenging thoughts and events, which considerably improves your wellbeing. By focusing on the present through mindfulness, you become less likely to get caught up in regrets over your past or worries over the future. You become less pre-occupied with the thoughts in your head and this generally improves your overall wellbeing.

3. IT IMPROVES PHYSICAL HEALTH

Apart from improving your mental wellbeing, research has also shown that mindfulness has a tremendous impact on physical health in numerous ways. Mindfulness relieves you of stress, anxiety, chronic pain, depression, and many other conditions that could be affecting your physical and mental health.

4. IT ENHANCES SLEEP

If you are being deprived of sleep from having to fight intrusive thoughts and having to perform compulsive behaviors, mindfulness meditation is there to help you start getting better sleep. Based on evidence, mindfulness has been shown to enable short-term improvement in the quality of sleep and in the mediation of sleep issues. Sleep deprivation is one of the things that worsen the OCD condition, so this is definitely a plus for you.

5. IT REDUCES STRESS

Intrusive thoughts can be really uncomfortable but that's not all, they can also increase your stress levels. Having to fight obsessions every day or perform compulsions is absolutely exhausting and draining, but when you make mindfulness a regular practice, you can easily relieve yourself of the stress you feel from having those intrusive thoughts. In fact, when it gets to a certain stage, you would no longer need to perform compulsions just to relieve yourself of the distress. Mindfulness is also very effective for altering the cognitive processes that bring about intrusive thoughts.

6. MINDFULNESS EASES PAIN AND ACHES

Ache and pain may develop from having to act out compulsions so many times in a day and being constantly stressed. Some of the pains we feel in the back, neck, and other body parts are in the mind, products of the battle we are constantly fighting with those uncomfortable alien thoughts. Thankfully, mindfulness can help ease those feelings and sensations of aches and pain you get. It appears that once you are able to bring relief and calm to your mind through mindfulness, these feelings also spread down to every part of your body.

7. IT ENHANCES MOODS

There is probably nothing better at improving moods than a mindfulness practice session, according to a recent study. A session of mindfulness in a highly tensed and stressful situation can really go a long way in shielding you from those emotions triggering your mood. In this case, mindfulness can serve as a sort of mental armor against those triggers.

8. IT IMPROVES FOCUS

Since this is what mindfulness is kind of about, it comes as no surprise that mindfulness can actually help increase focus in a person. When you regularly practice mindfulness, it becomes easier to concentrate on important things and disregard the distracting ones like your intrusive thoughts. This also improves overall performance at everything.

9. IT IMPROVES MENTAL HEALTH

Well, this is evidently obvious since we are talking about how to use mindfulness to manage symptoms of OCD. Psychotherapy professionals have adopted mindfulness meditation as an important technique in the treatment of varying mental health problems, anxiety disorders and OCD included.

10. MINDFULNESS IMPROVES QUALITY OF LIFE

This is an obvious one so what's there to talk about?

Overall, what you should know and accept is that mindfulness is a very important technique that you must embrace on your path to recovering from obsessive compulsive disorder. With the combination of mindfulness and CBT or any other effective OCD therapy, you can send intrusive obsessional thoughts and compulsive behaviors scuttling from your life.

CHAPTER NINE:
COGNITIVE BEHAVIORAL THERAPY

Cognitive behavioral therapy has been recognized and acknowledged as the most effective treatment therapy for obsessive compulsive disorder and this is because it involves evidence-based methods that are proven to change thoughts, feelings, behaviors, and ultimately result in optimal life satisfaction and functioning. Cognitive behavioral therapy (CBT) techniques have been developed based on the most recent psychological research, with repeated demonstrations of their effectiveness in treating social and mental disorders. Before we move on to talking about the different CBT techniques for OCD treatment, let's understand what CBT is in full.

Cognitive behavioral therapy is a form of psychotherapeutic treatment that aims to help patients understand the thoughts and feelings that influence their behaviors. Although it is a short-term therapy treatment, CBT helps people change their behaviors by modifying their thinking patterns. In short, CBT helps you learn to modify your thoughts and feelings so you can change whatever dysfunctional behavior you don't like and that is affecting your health and life.

Unlike the traditional Freudian psychoanalysis therapies which aim to understand past problems that developed from childhood so as to get to the root of a problem, CBT is centered on solutions that help people modify distorted cognitive processes and negative behavioral patterns. The whole concept of CBT is based on the idea that our behaviors are influenced by our thoughts and feelings. So if we can change our cognitive processes for the better, we can easily change and modify our behaviors. This explains why CBT is the most effective therapy technique for obsessive compulsive disorders since compulsions (behaviors) are influenced by obsessions (thoughts).

Different cognitive behavioral techniques help people combat stress and cope with many other negative life challenges. The most interesting and fascinating thing about CBT is that it is a goal-oriented approach that targets specific problems and requires a patient's active involvement for success. It is also time-based, which means you would know the period of time for which you will be having therapy and you would also be able to track your progress, based on what you expect.

The objective of CBT is to help you identify harmful

and negative thoughts, determine whether they are a true representation of your reality, and if they aren't, help you employ therapeutic strategies in overcoming these harmful thoughts. Evidence amounts to support the fact that CBT can actually help with a number of mental health conditions like OCD, PTSD, anxiety disorders, depressive disorders, eating disorders, and several others. In fact, research also exists to indicate that CBT sessions can be successfully delivered online, in conjunction with face-to-face sessions.

According to the American Psychology Association, CBT works on a number of beliefs that include:

- How thinking in unhelpful ways can result in psychological problems for people
- How learning unhelpful behavior can also result in psychological problems
- How people can learn and adopt more positive and beneficial ways of thinking
- How developing new habits can help people relieve symptoms of different mental and physical health problems and also enable them act more positively

CBT professionals and practitioners work on the theory that the problems we have in life, whether physical or mental, arise from the interpretation we give to our thoughts and the events happening in our lives. With obsessive compulsive disorder, CBT works specifically to help sufferers feel less fearful and anxious, without having to contend with obsessions or compulsions. There are five key things to know about CBT.

Compared to other talk therapy, CBT is ideal because it is **problem-specific and goal-oriented.** This means you can settle on a specific problem to tackle with a specific goal to achieve when it comes to CBT. For instance, if your problem is the checking OCD, your CBT therapy will be targeted specifically and only at achieving the goal of stopping the compulsive checking behaviors you exhibit. Once you solve this particular problem and achieve your goal, then you and your therapist can decide if there is still anything to work on or if you should just end treatment. If there is anything more to work on, then you begin a new time-limited CBT program with a specific problem and goal to achieve in mind.

Another ideal thing about CBT is that it **focuses on the present**. Cognitive behavioral therapy doesn't seek to dig up and understand the past, and neither does it concern itself with the future. Instead, it focuses on present problems and current events causing distress. This makes it easier for you to solve your problems faster and more effectively. Identifying a specific challenge and focusing solely on that in a structured therapy yields greater treatment results that are achieved faster than in other traditional talking therapies.

Cognitive behavioral therapy also **requires active effort from you** as the patient. You are expected to work collaboratively with your therapist so you can solve problems together. Instead of simply awaiting results and for your problems to get better just because you have talked to your therapist about them over and over, you have the opportunity to participate actively in your own treatment. With self-help assignments and other CBT tools you use between sessions, you can quicken the pace of your therapy and treatment process. Every session you have will focus on helping you identify thinking patterns from different perspectives and also help you unlearn unwanted behaviors and reactions.

CBT is **time-limited and brief**. What this means is that you have the choice to end treatment as soon as you experience considerable relief from symptoms of OCD and you already have all the skills required for further successful treatment of your symptoms. Thanks to this, CBT is briefer than other traditional talk therapies that sometimes last for years. There are people who finish their CBT therapy after only a few months of treatment. However, this is not to say that everyone makes significant progress in a short period of time. Depending on the mildness or severity of your symptoms, you may need to add more sessions of therapy for lasting change and reduction of symptoms. Since OCD is usually chronic, OCD sufferers may require between six months and several years of treatment. However, even in cases like this, CBT is simply more effective and shorter in duration than traditional talk therapy.

If you don't already know it, then know now that CBT is a **widely-researched technique** and this explains why it is very effective for solving mental health problems and conditions. More than 500 studies have been conducted on cognitive behavioral therapy and all studies attest to the effectiveness of CBT for several psychological and medical conditions. CBT is one of the few therapies that are scientifically and clinically proven to give effective solutions to problems. Cognitive behavioral therapy teaches you to:

> ➤ Develop self-awareness of automatic negative thoughts

- Identify your problems clearly
- Challenge and change underlying beliefs that are wrong
- Distinguish between reality and irrational ideas or thoughts
- Let go of your fear
- Develop a healthier and more positive approach to thinking and interpreting situations
- Concentrate on how things are instead of how they may turn out
- Face your fears rather than avoid or find a way around them
- Accept and understand yourself instead of judging

Cognitive behavioral therapy also incorporates a lot of learning tools to make your treatment achievable and these include:

- Regular individual or group discussions, or a mix of both
- Role playing
- Exercises to calm your mind and body
- Constant feedback
- Exposure exercises
- Homework assignments
- Cognitive behavioral journal or diary
- Skills to enhance positive, personal growth and development

The objective of cognitive behavioral therapy is to

help you transform thoughts and feelings that obstruct the achievement of positive outcomes. For instance, a typical OCD sufferer becomes disengaged with reality due to their obsessive thoughts. This distorted perception of reality makes them prone to a negative thinking pattern, overgeneralization, over-exaggeration of situations, and a white-or-black mindset. When your mind becomes preoccupied with obsessional thinking, it may lead you to adopt an automatic negative way of thinking. CBT will help you challenge the automatic negative thoughts so you can compare them with reality and see the true state of things for you. In a nutshell, CBT as a form of talking psychotherapy helps you challenge your fears and change your perception of reality so as to initiate positive effect on mind, body, and behaviors.

Since CBT is an umbrella under which there are different exercises, each exercise is best used for some specific psychological or medical problem. Cognitive behavioral therapy for OCD usually involves a combination of some of the following therapies or exercises:

- **Cognitive restructuring:** This is a treatment exercise where an OCD patients is taught to recognize unhelpful and unhealthy thinking patterns so he or she can change and replace them with more positive ways of thinking. With obsessive compulsive disorder, the aim of cognitive restructuring exercises is to help sufferers reduce anxiety-inducing interpretations and assumptions about obsessional thoughts and compulsive behaviors.

- **Activity scheduling:** This is a cognitive behavioral technique aimed at specifically helping people increase positive behaviors they should be doing more of. Activity scheduling helps a patient recognize and schedule healthy behaviors such as meditating, socializing so as to increase an individual's likelihood of getting that activity done or indulging in that behavior. This method is most effective for people with depressive disorders or procrastination since they usually find it difficult to get things done or do something they like. In short, activity scheduling will help you cultivate healthier and more positive behaviors that will significantly impact your health.

- **Successive approximation:** This is a cognitive behavioral therapy designed especially for people who find it difficult to get a task done for whatever reason. It involves helping patients master a less difficult task similar to the challenging or overwhelming task they have at hand.

- **Mindfulness meditation exercise:** This is an effective cognitive behavioral therapy technique for people with obsessive compulsive disorder and it is usually combined with exposure and response prevention. The technique was borrowed from Buddhism and is all about getting an OCD sufferer or any other person to disengage from rumination and obsession over negative, unhealthy things while redirecting their attention to whatever is happening in the present moment. Just like CBT, mindfulness is at the cutting-edge of psychotherapeutic analysis.

Based on evidence and practice, the most effective CBT exercises for treating OCD are a combination of Exposure Response Prevention (ERP) and mindfulness meditation exercise. Therefore, let's look at how a combination of these two exercises can help you treat and overcome your OCD.

EXPOSURE AND RESPONSE PREVENTION (ERP)

Also referred to as Exposure and Ritual Prevention, ERP is a specialized cognitive-behavioral therapy which works specifically for obsessive compulsive disorder and a range of related anxiety disorders. ERP is designed specifically to break the two recurring patterns that are associated with OCD. The first pattern is the association between feelings of distress and the thoughts, ideas, and situations that trigger the feelings of distress. The second one is the pattern between carrying out compulsive ritualistic behavior and decreasing feelings of distress.

ERP aims to break the link between feelings of distress and anxiety and ritualistic or compulsive behaviors. ERP also helps patients learn how not to perform rituals even when feelings of anxiety or fear are involved. Exposure and ritual prevention encompasses three different components in treatment. These are: vivo exposure, imaginary exposure, and ritual prevention.

Vivo exposure is a real life or actual exposure to feared thoughts, objects, or situations. It has to do with staying in the presence of a feared situation of object for a long period of time so as to evoke fearful and anxious feelings. Someone with contamination OCD may be exposed to a dirty surface or anything else that is a contaminant. Imaginary exposure is the process of mentally exposing OCD sufferers to feared thoughts, situations, or objects. The patient may also be exposed to the consequence of a feared situation, for example, mentally visualizing a car hitting a loved one and the death of the loved one. Ritual prevention involves stopping a patient from performing a ritualistic or compulsive behavior. For instance, touching a dirty surface without cleaning or washing the hands.

The first concept in Exposure Response Prevention is exposure. This is a procedure whereby you are made to purposely confront thoughts, ideas, objects, or events that trigger distress and then remain in that situation long enough for your feelings of distress and anxiety to diminish on their own. In vivo exposure for instance, patients are made to confront feared situation in reality, not in their heads. For instance, a person who is scared of hitting someone while driving would be made to drive long enough to diminish the feelings of anxiety and distress that come with having to drive. In a case like this, such a person may feel like the distress will never go if they don't avoid or escape the situation. They may also feel like they can't actually handle the situation. Contrary to their belief, they always end up discovering that this isn't true. At first, this person may experience distress, anxiety, and discomfort. But, with time and continual exposure practice, they would discover that the situations they so fear would no longer make them feel uncomfortable like it once did. This is what is referred to as 'habituation' in ERP.

If habituation occurs and works, you as the patient would end up wondering why you didn't think of relieving your distress by confronting the situations that provoked your obsessive thoughts and distress. However, provoking and confronting an obsession simply isn't enough. You must be exposed to the obsession long enough to get your distressful and anxious feelings to diminish on their own. In addition, exposure doesn't work just because you did it once, it must be repeated over and over for you to really see improvements in your OCD symptoms.

There are situations where you can't confront feared objects or situations or their perceived consequences through vivo exposure. For instance, if your OCD is the checking type and your fear is that your house may burn down if you do not constantly check to see if the stove is turned off or the iron is unplugged, it isn't possible for your house to be burned down or smart for the stove to be left on just to enable you confront your feared situation. This is where imaginary exposure comes to play. With imaginary exposure, the OCD patients is asked to confront the feared situation by visualizing it in their mind. Imaginal or imaginary exposure involves visualizing every detail of the perceived disaster in your mind with the use of images. Just like in vivo exposure, the distress from confronting the situation mentally gradually decreases in imaginal exposure too.

Imaginary exposure is also regarded as the most helpful exposure method for people who experience obsessive thoughts simultaneously, without any obvious trigger or identifiable situations. For example, some people experience intrusive, violent or blasphemous thoughts at any given time of place. This intrusive thought may then bring about distress. In this case, there is no obvious situation for the person to confront in real life and it isn't possible to practice being in the exposure situation for a long period of time. So using imaginary exposure, the situation can be mentally visualized over and over, without trying to suppress the thought or neutralize the distress with a ritual. Sometimes, imaginal exposure is also used to make subsequent vivo exposure practices easier for a patient. If your OCD is severe and you are extremely uncomfortable at the thought of confronting a feared object or situation in "real life," your therapist may suggest confronting it imaginarily first. The decrease in anxiety and distress you experience from the visualization process will extend over to the vivo exposure practices.

After successful exposure, the next concept in ERP is response prevention or ritual prevention, as it is also called. When people with obsessive compulsive disorder have obsessional thoughts of face feared situations, they become distressed and anxious to the point where performing certain compulsive or ritualistic behaviors is the only way they know to provide relief from the feelings of distress. When exposure is practiced too, it also evokes the same feeling of distress and an urge to act out compulsions. Therefore, in ERP, ritual prevention practice is used to help you break that habit of acting out compulsions. Response or ritual prevention has to do with learning to stop compulsions or rituals, even when the urge to do so is still there. Typically, compulsions are difficult to break or stop since they provide temporary relief from distress or anxiety. But, you are learning to stop compulsions not because they provide relief but because they are negative and dysfunctional ways of seeking relief; they interfere with your physical, mental, emotional, and social functioning. Through ritual prevention, you will learn to stop rituals and find more effective ways of coping with distress or anxiety.

If you have OCD or a loved one with OCD, Exposure and Ritual Prevention is the ideal CBT treatment exercise for obvious reasons. Note that we already said that the objective of ERP is to help you weaken or break the connections between the two recurring themes in OCD. Remember that like we said, the only reason you perform compulsions is because they provide temporary relief when you carry them out and this prompts you to continue to engage in the ritualistic behaviors. However, when you learn to not respond to obsessive thoughts with rituals, you are weakening or breaking the bond between compulsions and the relief from distress that they give you.

Apart from helping you to weaken or break the connections between the two associations, ERP is also designed to help erase common misconceptions or mistakes in OCD which trigger significant distress. The first of these misconceptions is that it is compulsory to avoid obsessive thoughts or perform rituals in order to prevent a perceived consequence. A major percentage of people have thoughts about potential disasters that may happen to them if they leave the stove on or when they are driving a car. However, because they can interpret these thoughts well enough to understand that the risk is low, they disable stress and ignore the thought. The reason why people with OCD become so distressed is because they are unable to rationally interpret the thought and make an informed judgment about how true or possible it is. To get rid of the uncomfortable feeling and also prevent harm, they start avoiding the thoughts or start ritualizing. This leaves no space for them to find out that the actual possibility of their feared situation ever happening and discover that the risks are very low. Exposure helps to correct this misconception. When you are exposed to a feared situation repeatedly without performing rituals, you find out that there was actually no possibility of harm in the first place. Thus, you learn that the possibility of risk is remote and you learn to ignore the obsessions as time goes on.

Example: Jon was afraid of contaminating germs

and falling ill, so he never used public restrooms no matter how pressed he was and always kept more than one hand soap in his bag. For ERP therapy, he practiced using public restrooms and having just one hand soap in his bag to wash with. After a straight 24 hours, he found that he was still very okay and using the public restroom and washing with just one hand soap had not affected his health. So, Jon learned that his fear of contamination was irrational and unfounded.

Another misconception and mistake that many people with OCD make is believing that not avoiding a distressing situation will leave them distressed forever. This compels them to start avoiding identified triggers and situations and to perform rituals whenever they couldn't avoid a situation. However, when exposure is practiced for prolong period of time, they discover that this isn't actually true. Anxiety doesn't persist; rather, it decreases when you remain in a distressful situation for long. If you face a distressing situation for about 1 to 2 hours, you will find yourself experiencing a gradual decrease in distress until the distress is no longer there. As the distress decreases, it becomes easier to see that the situation was never actually dangerous. When you find yourself in the same situation in future, you will surely experience lesser feeling of distress than you used to.

Example: Mary was afraid that her house would catch fire so she never used her central heating even in cold climates, whether she was around in the house or not. For ERP, she practiced leaving the central heating on while she stayed there in the house. After some hours, she found that her house was becoming comfortably warm and there was actually no fire breakout in the home. Thus, she learned that avoiding using her central heating was irrational because the risk rate is remote anyways.

The third common mistake people with OCD make which ERP helps to correct is believing that if they don't avoid the obsessive thoughts or act out compulsions, they would lose their mind from feeling so much distress. For instance, you may be constantly worried about not arranging things tidily; this probably makes you feel like the distress you feel from not being able to tolerate the disorganization may cause you to lose your mind and then you would end up in a home for psychiatric people. In this case, you may practice disorganizing your room without rearranging it no matter how much distress it makes you feel. In time, you will feel your distress diminishing even without you tidying up the room or rearranging the things. Through this, you will learn that being distressed or anxious can't possibly result in insanity or other mental challenges.

ERP with the prolonged exposure period is made to help you challenge your intrusive thoughts logically. One important thing you should know is that you need to be emotionally invested for the therapy to truly work for you. Emotional involvement is something that is required during exposure exercises, whether vivo or imaginal. Particularly, an exposure exercise must evoke the exact kind of obsessive distress you experience on a normal day. To encourage emotional involvement, your therapist should make sure the exposure exercises match the thoughts and situations that trigger your obsessions and make you perform compulsions. For example, if you have a fear of contracting HIV and you go to a hospital ward with no HIV patients, the exposure exercise will not help because that is not a feared situation to you. Thus, it will be hard for you to give an apt emotional response or be distressed when your exercise does not align with your obsessions.

Even when the exposure exercise aligns with your obsessions, you must make efforts to ensure that you involve yourself emotionally in the exercise. To do this, you must pay attention to the very things and details you find distressing in the feared situation instead of trying to ignore or avoid them. This is the case for both vivo and imaginal exposure exercises. For instance, if you act like an HIV ward is in fact a cancer ward just so you can minimize the distress during the exercise, then the exposure process won't be effective. Therefore, when practicing exposure, you must make sure you pay attention to the potential harm you are faced with by being in the feared situation. For example, when you go to a HIV ward with patients, to really involve your emotions, think about the things there that are most likely to give you HIV, such as the syringe, the blood, etc. In imaginal exposure, you should ensure you concentrate on imagining even the tiniest details just to make the visualization as a vivid as possible.

Now, looking at how easy and straightforward the whole process seems just by reading about it, you may feel like Exposure and Ritual Prevention is actually something you can do on your own to stop your OCD. You may think that simply giving up compulsive behaviors is enough and you wouldn't need to go for professional treatment. Many people with OCD can actually stop their avoidance and ritual behaviors for a while but it becomes uncomfortable in the period and they are unable to actually go through with the whole thing. Exposure just doesn't work like that. Of course, you may be able to square off with obsessions a number of times by confronting the situations you fear, but your OCD behaviors will likely persist. What you need is exercises that are designed and tailored to you, and you also have to do the exercises correctly. Trained psychotherapists are the best people to design your exposure and Ritual Prevention exercises, and will be there to be your coach and guide as you practice exposure and response prevention. It isn't recommended that you practice ERP on your own because you may end up worsening your symptoms.

Exposure and ritual prevention can be very effective, especially when it is combined with mindfulness meditation. However, the results you get depend on the effort you put into the therapeutic sessions. It also depends heavily on the ability of your therapist to come up with an exposure plan that is tailored to your OCD symptoms; this is why it is very important that you approach a licensed and trained professional only. Even when your exposure exercises seem counterintuitive or over-the-top, remember that you have to overlook that and put in the effort. The goal of ERP therapy isn't to help you start acting and behaving like a "non-OCD" person; rather, it is to help you weaken and possibly break the hold your obsessions and compulsions have on you.

Exposure and Response Prevention may appear extremely challenging for you at times and this is understandable. It takes a lot of hard work and willpower to confront situations that distress you so much. But know that it is necessary to practice exposure so to reduce your anxiety and discomfort without having to result to compulsions. The more you practice exposure, the easier the exercises become and the freer you are from obsessional thoughts and compulsive ritualistic behaviors.

PROS AND CONS OF COGNITIVE BEHAVIORAL THERAPY FOR OCD PATIENTS

Combined with medication, cognitive behavioral therapy has a lot of advantages for people suffering from OCD and other anxiety/depression disorders. Just like everything else, CBT has its disadvantages, which aren't really disadvantages, depending on your perspective.

Firstly, cognitive behavioral therapy can be just as effective as medication in the treatment of obsessive compulsive disorder. In fact, when combined with OCD medications, CBT can be really effective within a short period of time.

Due to the highly structured nature of CBT, you can choose to engage in your sessions using various formats ranging from group therapies to self-help books and computer programs. The choice is really all yours.

Again, every skill you learn during your CBT sessions can be incorporated into your everyday life to help you manage future challenges and difficult situations, even after treatment has ended.

However, to benefit from the numerous advantages of CBT, you must be able to commit yourself fully to the process. CBT isn't like traditional psychotherapy where the therapist did more of the problem solving. If you really want your problems to go away using CBT, you must be ready to cooperate fully with your therapist.

Another things is CBT is meant to be practiced for a brief period of time so regular sessions and home assignments can really take up a lot of your time, leaving just a little space for other activities. Also, the structured nature of CBT makes it unsuitable for people with learning difficulties or complicated health needs.

Some people argue that since CBT is problem-specific and only addresses current situations, it is not as effective because that doesn't address underlying causes of mental health problems like childhood and upbringing.

Conclusively, CBT concentrates on the individual and their capacity for initiating change in themselves. Therefore, it doesn't help to understand wider problems and external factors that may be impacting an individual's physical and mental wellbeing.

These little 'cons'aside, you can see that cognitive behavioral therapy has a lot of pros to help you deal with your disorder. With an adequate amount of effort and diligence from you, you'd find yourself faster on your path to recovery from OCD. Before we go on to talk about how you can move on with life after OCD recovery, let's find out about some of the best, medically-proven medications for OCD treatment.

BEST MEDICATIONS FOR THE TREATMENT OF OBSESSIVE COMPULSIVE DISORDER

Cognitive behavioral therapy is recommended as the primary form of treatment for obsessive compulsive disorder, but adding the use of OCD medications to the process could bring more benefits to you. Normally, medication isn't ideal as a sole treatment for OCD but in practice, people are often allowed to get started on medication while they remain in the long waiting line for psychotherapy. In this case, it should be your choice to decide if you would prefer to start using medication or not. You can either choose medication, CBT, or a combination of both which is actually more effective for treatment. While it isn't advisable to start treatment solely on medication due to the possibility of suffering a relapse, if you have depression and low mood due to your OCD, then medication may be an ideal choice for you since this is known to help a lot of people with moods and depressive disorders, both of which are side effects of OCD. There are many reasons why you shouldn't consider using medication as your sole method of treatment for OCD. The first is that CBT treatment is more effective and it lasts way longer. It is also less expensive than medication and does not have any known side effects, by the way. Studies have also shown that people are less likely to suffer relapse from treatment when they use CBT, unlike medication, which makes people suffer relapse a lot.

The good thing about medication is that it could serve as an appetizer to the main course, which is cognitive behavioral therapy. Meditation may help reduce distress and anxiety long enough for you to get started on CBT and eventually succeed with your therapy sessions. The medication you use before you start CBT will of course help but what will help you achieve lasting results is all the skills you garner from your cognitive behavioral exercises.

The main medication used for the treatment of OCD comes in the form of anti-depressants which help target serotonin pathways in the brain and they are usually referred to as Selective Serotonin Re-uptake Inhibitor or,SSRIs for short. Like you learned in an earlier chapter, there is no known reason as to why SSRIs are effective for some people with OCD. However, experts think that they could be impacting the balance of chemicals in the brain and this may be responsible for the effects and change. What is confirmed though is that SSRIs reduce the symptoms of obsessive compulsive disorder, depending on the severity. The most popular, longest used, and clinically-backed medication for OCD is an SSRI known as Anafranil. But, there are tons of other medications, both on-label and off-label, which you can use for treatment.

Some medications are approved by the Food and Drug Administration (FDA) for the treatment of OCD in both kids and adults. Most of these medications are SSRI but Anafranil falls into a class of medications known as the tricyclic antidepressants. The FDA-approved medications include:

- Anafranil (clomipramine): This is a medication that has long been in use for the treatment of OCD. It is approved by the FDA for treatment of OCD in adults and kids ages 10 years+. As effective as it is, anafranil also has more side effects than any other anti-depressants. This has resulted in SSRIs being the more recommended medication for OCD since they typically have fewer side effects.
- Prozac (fluoxetine): This is a type of SSRI that works to increase the level of serotonin in neural pathways. Prozac is effective for treatment in adults and children ages 7 years and above. It typically comes in capsule form.
- Luvox (fluvoxamine): Another SSRI that performs the same function as Prozac. It is recommended for treatment in adults and kids ages 8 and above. It comes in tablet and extended-release capsule forms.

- Zoloft (sertraline): Meant for treating OCD in adults and children ages 6 and above, Zoloft is another FDA-approved medication that comes in liquid and tablet forms.
- Paxil (paroxetine): This is also an FDA-approved SSRI anti-depressant that is used for OCD treatments in adults only. Paxil only comes in liquid and tablet forms.

There are also off-label medications which have been proven effective in the treatment of OCD but are not yet approved by the FDA. Some off-label medications are SSRI and also Serotonin and Norepinephrine reuptake inhibitors (SNRIs) may be prescribed by your physician even though they are off-label. They include: Celexa (citalopram), Lexapro (escitalopram), and Effexor (venlafaxine). Duloxetine (Cymbalta) is another SNRI anti-depressant which may be prescribed for OCD treatment. In some people, SNRIs are often found to be more effective than SSRIs, with fewer side effects.

There are times when a person with OCD may also be prescribed a drug known as benzodiazepine. This medication is very effective for reducing anxiety but there is not enough proof to show that it really is effective for the treatment obsessive compulsive disorder. Also, patients are likely to develop a tolerance to the medication and in certain cases, become addicted. Discontinued use of benzodiazepines may also lead to strong withdrawal symptoms in some people. Benzodiazepines are usually prescribed with SSRIs until the SSRI reaches full effect. This medication is not appropriate for long-term use.

Note that when you are prescribed any OCD treatment medication, it is important and compulsory that you use the medication exactly as it was prescribed to you. Whatever class of antidepressant is prescribed to you, know that experiencing their full effect may take up to numerous weeks and even months sometimes. If there are any side effects, you should immediately consult with your doctor or physician. Also, never stop using an OCD medication without guidance or direction from your doctor so as to avoid having withdrawal symptoms. The most common side effects of OCD medications include:

- Nervousness
- Insomnia
- Dry mouth
- Nausea
- Dizziness
- Drowsiness
- Migraines

- ➢ Diarrhea
- ➢ Erectile dysfunction
- ➢ Loss of sexual appetite
- ➢ Blurry vision

Usually, side effects vanish some weeks after you start medication but if they persist, your doctor may link you up with another medication. Notwithstanding, it is extremely important that you keep track of side effects so you can notify your doctor immediately there is an emergency. Also, make sure you talk about other medications you may be using or any other medical conditions you have before you start taking any medication for OCD.

If you have OCD and you are pregnant or you have plans to get pregnant, ensure you talk with a doctor about the health risks and benefits of taking OCD medication. Some SSRI medications such as Zoloft and Prozac can be taken during pregnancy.

Combining cognitive behavioral therapy with medication is the ideal thing to do but if you would rather take medications, remember that there is a higher possibility of experiencing relapse and the solution won't be as lasting and effective. With the right treatment, tools, and support from people you love, you can recover fully from OCD and get started with "life after recovery," which could be a little dreadful at first. How? Find out for yourself in the next chapter!

CHAPTER TEN:
RECOVERY FOR LIFE

The goal of anybody with any mental health condition is to find the proper treatment and tools they need to get started on the path to recovery. It is quite challenging to find the right therapist, capable of giving you the proper treatment you seek, to go through exposure and response prevention, use your medications, and reach a point where you can say assuredly that you have "recovered" from OCD. But really, after treatment, does recovery just happen like that? What happens after treatment? Do you just go back to living your life like you never had to deal with OCD? What kind of life do you even plan to live after your OCD treatment and recovery? These are the important questions that require pondering while you are undergoing your OCD treatment.

As OCD patients get better and see their symptoms improve, it is normal to become relieved that distress is no longer a constant part of their lives and they don't have to perform compulsions again; they can now get back to living a normal life. Of course, this is a happy thing considering that this was the goal of seeking treatment to that life-stressing disorder in the first place. However, most patients often come to realize that feelings of grief take the place of those past feelings of anxiety and distress after treatment has been completed. This may come as a surprise because why would anybody miss or grieve over a life they wish they never had in the first place? Can you really call that a recovery then? While the definition of recovery may be specific to an individual perspective on recovery, there is still a generally accepted definition of recovery. According to the dictionary, recovery is "restoration to health from sickness."

So, can you really be said to have recovered from OCD if you grief over the absence of its symptoms in your life? Usually, what happens with people who are able to treat and 'recover' from OCD is that they have spent a lot of their lives struggling with obsessions and engaging in compulsive behaviors that consume a huge part of their lives. Their lives have been altered by OCD to a point where they don't know what a 'normal' life should feel like anymore. Of course, it's not that they like having the disorder but it's been there for such a long time that it has become a part of them and they don't feel absolutely 'complete' without the presence. Some people even wonder what they would have to think about if the obsessions weren't there anymore, disregarding the fact that there are millions of positive things to think about. Getting back your life from OCD may seem like a dreadful experience at first. Feeling better may even make you feel anxious since you aren't used to feeling 'well.' You aren't used to not being consumed by your obsessions.

In case you feel like this when you finally start recovering, what you must know is that it is normal and common to feel a sense of loss; it doesn't take anything away from your recovery. If you aren't careful, OCD may try to wiggle its way back into your life because all those worries you have about the life to come are a potentially fertile ground for OCD to try and breed on. However, what you can do to ensure that your recovery is one for life is to talk with your psychotherapist and make a list of everything and every experience you believe you have missed out on while you contended with the obsessions and compulsions. Describe every one of those things you would love to catch up on for your therapist and then make a list. Then, your therapist can work on incorporating these things into your CBT plan and life as your OCD symptoms diminish, probably using the activity scheduling exercise.

While doing this, ensure you aren't aggravating and

inviting your OCD symptoms back. Some unassuming family members may trigger this in their bid to show you extraordinary care and attentions while you recover, not knowing it may lead to a relapse. Find ways of engaging with loved ones and other people around without talking of OCD or trying to seek reassurance from them. It may have been difficult to engage other thoughts or things that excite you and make you happy while your mind was being occupied by OCD. But remember that you are in charge completely now and you do not need to be defined by your OCD.

Live life the way you want, not the way OCD would have had you live life if it was still there. Identify your goals in life and start working towards them, within the framework of your beliefs and value system. Adopt gratitude as your new way of life and make sure you are as excited about your new life as you should be. To further brighten your life and ensure you are living it the positive way, incorporate all of the ten tips below into your life!

TIPS FOR LIVING A HEALTHIER, HAPPIER AND MORE POSITIVE LIFE

Living a healthy, happy, and positive life seems like such a simple thing but it's not easy. After recovery, it is vital that you live your life to the fullest and catch up on all the fun, excitement, and experiences you missed out on while still battling your disorder. But now that the OCD life may be over, how should you start living life ahead? Here are ten helpful tips for you.

1. **Be yourself:** The most vital thing anybody that wants to be happier and healthier to know is that it pays to be oneself. The power of accepting yourself and feeling comfortable in your own skin cannot be underestimated. Any situation you find yourself in, accept it as it is. Understand that it is who you are and there is no point trying to change yourself. The inability to accept oneself and practice self-love is the foremost happiness killer. Not being comfortable in your own skin can kill your self-esteem, confidence, and the happiness that is supposed to shine from within you. The most important relationship you can ever have is the one you have with yourself and you have to ensure it is a happy and positive one because you know what? Nobody would care for you like you would for yourself. Never judge yourself for anything, be it your appearance, education, or background. Stay away from shallow-minded and judgmental people so they don't pollute your mindset and upset your happiness.

2. **Appreciate what you have:** True happiness can never be acquired if all you do is worry about what you wish you had or if you keep comparing yourself with others. The grass may appear greener on the other side but is it really greener? If you never express contentment with your life and what you have, you will find yourself living a life of misery, with a hollowness in your heart. Never let other people be your benchmark of success; it can result in depression and mood disorders. Live life acknowledging and appreciating whatever you have and you will find yourself basking in an aura of joy and happiness every day.

3. **Always see a positive side of any situation:** No matter what you do, you will always face challenges and unfriendly situations. Challenges are a part of life so this shouldn't come as a surprise. When faced with unpleasant situations, you can choose to be sad, angry, depressed, or anxious about the situation or you can choose to look at the brighter side and turn it around to focus on just the positive. Avoid letting negativity become a loophole in your life ever again. Take every lesson with a smile and every setback as an opportunity for you to grow. Train your mind to be stronger so you can deal with whatever life throws at you.

4. **Get rid of the need to control:** Control is a human way of seeking security but control can also make you insecure. When you have a need to control your life and the situations you find yourself in, it is because you need to feel more secure. But, in the same sense, you can lose control just by feeling more secure. This comes as a result of being dependent on the feeling of control. This can make you go ballistic and crazy when things go out of your control. Having a need for control will push people away from you and leave you feeling more depressed than usual.

5. **Live in the present:** Forget about the regrets of the past or the uncertainties of the future. Bury yourself in the moment and live it to the fullest. One of the reasons why children are always so happy is because they live in and for the moment. You should endeavor to focus solely on what is happening with you presently and not what happened in the past or what may happen in the future. When you allow yourself live in the moment, you open yourself to boundless feelings of joy and happiness.

6. **Do not overanalyze:** Overanalyzing is one of the reasons why many people experience anxiety and depression; it is also one of the

things that complicate symptoms of OCD sometimes. Stop overanalyzing the events in your life and whatever situations you find yourself in. From school or work to relationships and finances, resist the urge to overanalyze any situation. Overanalyzing is when you chew over and over on something, trying to get to the root just because you perceive that may give you a way out. However, overanalyzing never provides a way out. Instead, it gives you the comfort you need to settle yourself gently into a nest of worries and doubts. Taking things in their stride and as they come while paying attention to your intuition is the way to go.

7. **Quit worrying about the future:** Worries about the future can often get overwhelming. We humans tend to worry about a lot of things, from health to career to love, we have a lot of worries. The one reason why we have so many worries is because we are scared and anxious. However, since worrying doesn't ever help or solve anything, then what's the need to spend so much time doing it? Quit worrying and spend that time engaging in more productive things and activities that would make your life better, happier, and more positive. Ensure that you are moving in the

right direction in life and concentrating on what makes you happy.

8. **Be open to change:** Having a narrow and shallow mind is the worst thing that can happen to anybody. It is important that you have an open mind that encourages change and flexibility. Don't be the type that stands rigidly on their beliefs and ideas no matter how skewed they seem. Be open to changing your beliefs when there is a need and place for it. Accept and respect others' beliefs too without superimposing your own beliefs on them. Ensure the idea of changes makes you feel comfortable and positive. Don't fight to accept others.

9. **Let go of your ego:** Without caution, you can become an unsuspecting victim of your ego. Your ego could take control your life and distort your perception of reality. You begin to live in an illusion created by your ego. Whether it is to make you feel happy or for any other reason, learn to drop your ego and be true to yourself and others around you.

10. **Do what makes you feel alive:** There is absolutely no point living life if you aren't doing what makes you feel happy and alive. Engage in activities that set you alive, spend

time with people radiating positivity, and generally revel in that freedom you finally have from OCD.

CONCLUSION

Congratulations, you made it to the end! It sure must have been a long read for you but without doubt, you have learned enough to transform your life around from the negative and depressive state it is right now to a bright, cheerful and positive life radiating of happiness and joy.

OCD is not an insurmountable condition and this is what we have been able to thoroughly explain in this book. Throughout the book, we have successfully examined everything there is to know about obsessive compulsive disorder. In the book, we have looked at the length and breadth of what OCD is and how you can make a full, successful recovery from this disorder.

As promised, you have learned a lot about how you can get intrusive thoughts and ritualistic behaviors to stop disrupting your physical and mental functioning in life. You have also learned all about the processes involved in cognitive behavioral technique and what you should expect from therapy. With everything you have learned in the book, it is safe to say that you are ready to seize control of your life, take it back from OCD and start your journey into a life of absolute calm, devoid of stress, anxiety, unhappiness, or depression.

RECOMMENDED RESOURCES

Want to learn more? We would like to recommend some amazing resources that will help you in your journey.

Go to the below URL for more details:

https://bit.ly/tmb-resources

Printed in Great Britain
by Amazon